# INSTRUCTIONAL DESIGN
# AND THE
# MEDIA PROGRAM

## William E. Hug

American Library Association          Chicago 1975

Library of Congress Cataloging in Publication Data
Hug, William E.
  Instructional design and the media program.
  Includes bibliographies.
  1. Media programs (Education).   2. Curriculum planning.
  I. Title.
LB1028.4.H83    375'.001    75-40425
ISBN 0-8389-0207-3

Printed in the United States of America

*To Kathy*

# CONTENTS

# FIGURES

# TABLES

# PREFACE

THE PURPOSE of INSTRUCTIONAL DESIGN AND THE MEDIA PROGRAM is to assist school and district media professionals, school administrators, and teachers in their efforts to conceptualize and build media programs as an integral part of the school curriculum. Thus, the book's content supports the movement away from the limited perception of the school library as a place offering a restricted number of services and the movement toward a more comprehensive view of the media program. This more comprehensive view stresses the value of the instructional design process as both art and science and the power of communication technology. Throughout the book media programs are viewed as vital to all aspects of the curriculum, and media professionals are seen as helping learners find, utilize, generate, and evaluate information from many sources, in numerous formats, and on different levels of difficulty.

More specifically, INSTRUCTIONAL DESIGN AND THE MEDIA PROGRAM may be used by college and university educational programs preparing media specialists and other media professionals, as well as by practitioners in the field. The content develops a philosophical and operational base for merging the school media program with a diversified curriculum. Several guides for teaching and learning alternatives for independent study, small group interaction, and class size groups are provided. For example, in each chapter there is a section on "Implications for the Media Program" which presents a summary of the key ideas and issues. Next, a section entitled "Problems and Activities for Research and Discussion" lists questions, problems, and other activities that can be utilized in individual and group activities. Finally, the "Sample Minimodule" at the end of each chapter illustrates other activities that can be developed around themes presented.

Each "minimodule" represents a mode of inquiry that can be used in a variety of ways. A mode of inquiry is a method or an instructional strategy employed to gain knowledge, a skill, or a competency. Other modes of inquiry or instructional strategies are introduced throughout the text to encourage the use of a wide range of instructional alternatives to which media programs must relate.

In many instances the chapters represent an expansion of the philosophy and procedures implied by both *Media Programs: District and School* (American Association of School Librarians, American Library Association and Association for Educational Communications and Technology, 1975) and *Guidelines for Two-Year College Learning Resources Programs* (*College & Research Libraries News*, no. 11, Dec. 1972). Both "standards" seem to assign the instructional design function to the media program with little attention to the retraining necessary for practitioners in the field. The discussions in this book of the role of media professionals and of the functions of the media program should help professionals as they strive to bridge the gap between the realities and expectations of the field.

Practitioners can use the material to assess their role in the educational program and to anticipate potential areas for personal and program growth and improvement. Many ways and means of interrelating the media program with the curriculum are offered to assist media professionals as they justify functions and operations to school administrators. The intent is to illustrate the actual and emerging role of the media specialist in the media program and of the media program in the curriculum. The role described focuses on the potential contribution of the media program and the subsequent realigning of priorities needed to move traditional concepts of school library service toward media programs that are more actively involved with students and the curriculum.

The first two chapters focus on what society expects of the schools and how educators respond. Chapter 1, "Information and the Mission of Education," discusses the nature of information, the kinds and value of information, and the role it plays in educational programs. The text argues that the demands of society have been relatively consistent and that the appropriate response of the profession has been toward an increased use of more scientific procedures. The movement toward more scientific procedures for decision making is generally referred to as technological responsibility.

The demands of society, the response of the profession, and the modes of inquiry introduced in the first chapter represent more stable elements than the "General Curriculum Movements" of chapter 2. Here the broad and frequently diffuse nature of each movement is considered, each one representing a different emphasis which tends to encourage or discourage the development of the more stable and hopeful elements. Each general curriculum movement is summarized, contrasted, and compared to others in order to demonstrate the influence they had and are having on educational and media programs. Those movements that have endured tend to have a more thoroughly developed base in both research and practice and are separated from the more philosophical movements that had little or no impact on the day-to-day routine observed in the classroom. Nevertheless, all movements represent different philosophical positions of today's school personnel, thus influencing their priorities and consequently encouraging certain kinds of programs. For this reason educators need to be aware of each curriculum movement.

Chapter 3, "Toward a Total Design," uses general systems theory—the study of a total system—as a way of organizing an educational system, taking into account the lessons of the past (chapter 2) and the assumptions about information (chapter 1). Chapter 3 applies systems principles to the building of an educational program that fuses the media program to the school curriculum. The material is built on the successes and failures of the past, those elements that seem to endure, and the more scientific processes developed by general systems theory.

As media professionals apply the principles of general systems theory, the functions and operations of the media program in relation to the school curriculum emerge. Chapter 4, "Interface between the School Media Program and the Curriculum," presents a typical group of functions and operations for building a media program that provides both the ways and means for educational program improvement.

The final chapter, "Technology as Means," introduces the more futuristic concept of technology as a process or means. In order to move forward with greater security, media personnel need to apply these processes. They represent the current technological thrust employed in educational programs and establish a common base for communicating with other educational professionals. Many of these processes have impact directly on the individual in the day-to-day contact media professionals have with users.

Throughout the text a plea is made for rational, democratic procedures for decision-making. In order to develop logical, purposeful educational and media programs, consideration is given to the obligation of the schools to fulfill society's goals and to provide an equal opportunity for each student, and to the obligation of the profession to actively and objectively explore more effective and efficient means of identifying both purpose and procedure.

Media programs change as a result of people viewing programs in new and different ways. The views held by communication technologists, librarians, instructional designers, systems engineers, curriculum workers, administrators, community members, teachers, and students can all contribute to the building of more purposeful and comprehensive media programs.

Professionals on all levels are encouraged to increase their understanding of the individual needs of each student. Greater sensitivity to the student enables professionals to apply their talent better and to grow in their vision of what the future can hold. Ultimately, the power to orchestrate a more individualized educational program depends upon the use of a wide range of appropriate alternatives that professionals know well enough to provide.

*All the business of life is to endeavour*
*to find out what you don't know by what*
*you do.*

THE DUKE OF WELLINGTON

# Information and the Mission of Education

INFORMATION IS a source of energy that enables a culture to perpetuate itself and to transcend that which is. The availability of information, the degree to which new information is generated, and the way it is used define the creative parameters of a culture. In this sense, education consists of developing a population that can find, evaluate, utilize, and generate information.

Educational systems need the information which will both accurately portray the role the culture expects the schools to play and will enable the systems themselves to make effective and efficient responses. For example, a democracy requires self-actualized, acculturated individuals, citizens who develop their potential and who contribute positively to society. In response to the needs of society, educational programs must have the information to translate needs into educational purposes and to develop more specific objectives as well as the ways and means of achieving them. The profession must apply principles of *best educational practice* and *technological responsibility* to the establishment of systems capable of building educational programs from these objectives.

Best educational practice implies possession of competencies that assist *media professionals* as they work with users—students, teachers, administrators, and the community. (As used herein, media professionals include all media personnel qualifying by education and position as professional. A media specialist is one kind of media professional.) Best educational practice, the art of the profession, includes principles and techniques media professionals apply on the spot to the day-to-day con-

1

tacts they have with users. Although much scientific planning may precede a particular activity, each activity usually requires the art of "pulling it off." Consequently, best educational practice is observed and evaluated as media professionals are working with users. In the preparation of media professionals, best educational practice is developed through activities, such as role playing and apprenticeships, that assist students in relating theory to application, subject content to the immediate environment, and self to society. Best educational practice includes the art of establishing rapport and providing information and assistance through the constant interchange professionals have with students, teachers, administrators, and other media program users.

Technological responsibility is the scientific application of laws and principles in the systems and instructional design process and in evaluation procedures. Scientific application requires a knowledge of facts, laws, and processes gained through study and practice. A *law* is a kind of rule supported by evidence collected through research and experience; a law is applied because information exists that suggests the degree of the law's effectiveness under specific conditions. A law may be expressed as an if-then type of statement: *If* a media program names specific objectives, *then* the products (benefits to users) of the media program can be assessed. *If* the precise requirements for a piece of communication equipment are listed, *then* the media professional can make intelligent choices among the commercial products available. *If* the media specialist desires to communicate the changing shape of an amoeba, *then* a combination of motion pictures, still visuals, and verbal explanation is required. In summary, a law is a statement of a process, order, or relationship that is known to exist under given circumstances, and technological responsibility is the systematic application of that which is known.

Technological responsibility is a cost-effective, process-product (if-then) approach to the solution of educational problems. In order to be cost-effective, the media program must prove its value to the educational program. Cost-effective programs justify expenditures in terms of the benefits (products) accrued to media program users. The changing processes used for budgeting are a case in point. Traditionally, budgets listed objects and expenditures. Today, budgets applying cost-benefit analyses in order to justify cost-effectiveness are program budgets, performance budgets, Planning, Programming and Budgetary Systems (PPBS), formula budgeting, and combinations. Technologically responsible systems strive to employ the most effective and efficient people-process-machine-material mixes supported by hard evidence which is frequently determined through statistical inference. Since knowing is essential to identifying and selecting alternatives that increase the probability of a system's success, the capacity to collect, to evaluate, to utilize, and to generate needed data is critical. Consequently, technological responsibility includes making decisions based on analysis, synthesis, and application of complete, relevant, and reliable information.

The way information is obtained, identified, and utilized to bring about learning is called the *mode of inquiry*. In modes of inquiry that stress social interaction, such as role playing, case studies, and sensitivity training, individuals are the primary information source. More traditional forms of media provide the primary information source in modes that assist students to find and comprehend the organization of a subject such as history or geology and that develop inductive and deductive reasoning. The environment provides basic information in developing competencies such as surveying a piece of land, observing and recording ecological changes, and developing the ability to utilize information resources of a given community. Historical, action, experimental, and other types of research may also be considered modes of inquiry.

A carefully selected, artfully articulated, and readily accessible collection of information resources is essential if each mode is to realize its full potential. What is important is that the informational support be suitable to the mode of inquiry. For example, a media specialist needs a media center, not an archive, for his apprenticeship; environmental structure will be his primary information source. In another instance, modes stressing social process would defeat their purposes if students were programmed individually through materials without the opportunity for interpersonal relationships.

### CHARACTERISTICS OF INFORMATION

Information takes numerous forms. For example, information may be in the form of body language, a symbol system that communicates in many subtle ways: a red face may indicate embarrassment, trembling may mean fear, applause may express approval, a frown may show disapproval. Aural symbols such as fire and ambulance sirens and visual symbols such as highway signs and mathematical equations also constitute information. Information scientists are concerned with the accurate and efficient transmission of information regardless of what it is rather than making value judgments about its quality. In this sense, information theory is not concerned with information as it is related to message content. However, media centers, media programs, and media specialists have a much different concern—they must deal with information in terms of content. Media specialists expend a large portion of their energy in the determination of the quality, appropriateness, and sources of information as it relates to the objectives of the educational program.

One kind of information exists in the way entities are arranged. For example, four parallel lines of equal length are known only by their relationship to each other. They could have a different relationship and form a square. These same four lines could also form the letters T V. Understanding how the lines or components of a system are "communicating" with one another provides necessary information for conceptualizing the whole.

Information may also be considered the content of a communication. In one sense, information is in the signal—the input to a receiver. Shannon and Weaver specify the components of a communication as (1) source, (2) transmitter, (3) signal, (4) receiver, and (5) destination.[1] This, like any model, is necessarily a summary of what is, a kind of shorthand which may be expressed in many ways. Berlo, for example, not only uses some different terms in describing the communication process but also extends the number of elements to include (1) source, (2) encoder, (3) message, (4) channel, (5) decoder, and (6) receiver.[2] Thus learning by using a book occurs in this manner: the author serves as the information source, all of the skills and technology needed to set the information on the page comprise the encoding process, light reflected from the page is the channel carrying the signal (information), and the eye translates the signal into another type of signal (nervous impulse) which is received and processed by the brain.

The brain may be defined as an information processing organ. However, the capacity of man's perceptual system is contingent on more than the ability to process information. It is also dependent upon experiential background. Learners must receive the necessary information and then be able to sort critical information from extraneous input to achieve efficiency. Media specialists must work through a similar process to exclude confusing, unnecessary, and irrelevant information.

A cold mass of air, the echo from a canyon wall, the fragrance of a flower, the blast of a fog horn, falling leaves, a paragraph in a book, and the holes in a Hollerith card all provide information. In fact, there does not seem to be any natural way to identify what provides information and what does not without being both artificial and arbitrary. As far as media programs are concerned, information can be defined simply as meaningful sensory input. This does not include such information exchanges as occur between materials and machines (magnetic tape and a tape re-

---

[1] Claude Shannon and Warren Weaver, *The Mathematical Theory of Communication* (Urbana: Univ. of Illinois Pr., 1949), p. 5.

[2] David K. Berlo, *The Process of Communication* (New York: Holt, Rinehart and Winston, 1960), p. 32.

corder) or machines and machines (Hollerith card and a computer). The primary concern of media programs is the *interface*—the point of information exchange between and among students, media specialists, teachers and other resources, machines, processes, and environments.

With these perceptions of both information and interfacing, a program may be described in terms of student (user) behaviors. The kind of behavior change observed is brought about by the purposeful, scientific, and artful articulation of *media program components*—people, materials, machines, processes, and environments that interface to form the program. The purpose of the media program is to assist individuals in the attainment of both personal and program objectives; the media program and the curriculum are instruments for changing behavior. Scientific and artful articulation of media program components refers to the concepts of technological responsibility and best educational practice.

Thus, media programs not only provide the information necessary for students to achieve personal and curricular objectives, but they also provide environments that encourage students to interact, confer, share, care, think, and challenge. Each activity relates to the way people are interfacing with each other, ideas, and processes as well as with physical objects such as materials, machines, and furniture.

Another view of information may be gained by observing the usefulness of a particular piece of information. Redundant information may equal no information. For example, the word "cherries" can be communicated by both print and sound. If both forms are present, one is providing no information. However, it is important to note that the first time a learner encounters "cherries," information may be provided by pictures, words, sound, and/or the cherries themselves. Perhaps a better example is a person who asks the advice of another. If the advice received is already known, the person received no information.

The concept of redundant information equaling no useful information has many implications for media programs, the most important one involving the tying of programs to the needs of the user population. Providing things without careful consideration to whether or not they supply needed information is obviously poor practice. Closely associated with this concept is the notion of information as something that reduces anxiety. For example, if a person is not sure how to mix gas and oil for his outboard motor, finding the formula reduces his anxiety. In this example, the formula represents the needed information. If, in a search for a new automobile route from Chicago to St. Louis, one finds the only routes are those traveled before, no useful information has been received (except, perhaps, that there is no other route).

A message, then, may or may not contain needed information. Thinking in these terms is important to the media specialist because such reasoning encourages a consideration of the interrelationships between what a message could contain, what a message does contain, and what the user needs. The kind and the quantity of information in a message must be linked to an understanding of the kind and amount of information needed to fill a specific information request. The choices made by the sender of a message are controlled by the number of possibilities at the sender's disposal. *The critical linkages are between that which can be transmitted and that which is transmitted, between that which is transmitted and that which is needed.*

The concept of education as a system which facilitates the processing of sensory input or information may be considered as part of the general field of *cybernetics*. Cybernetics is essentially concerned with the regulation and control of automated systems through the storing, transmitting, and processing of information. In the broadest sense, cybernetics is the science of interactions, especially as cybernetic theory relates to information exchange.[3] An interesting point concerning both cybernetic and general systems theory is that each system must exist for a specified purpose and must be limited to the purposes identified. The danger to society, not to mention students themselves, rests in the establishment of purposes for educational systems which are at variance with those needed by society for its own survival.

The value of an instructional system may be thought of in terms of the amount of useful information transmitted by that system. Information is a basic component of both knowledge and instruction and may consist of discrete bits, whereas knowledge (synthesis of information–experience) has more structure. The human mind is capable of organizing bits of information into knowledge by integrating and relating the information to previous experience. Instruction is a process designed to change or expand what a student feels, knows, and understands, while information retrieval systems simply yield bits of information for a user without concern for what is to be done with the information retrieved. In the process of instructional design, information is retrieved and organized into an instructional system for the purpose of producing learning.[4]

The practitioners in the field must know if they are providing needed information. If they know how and why a communication takes place, they may be able to determine what will meet the informational needs of

---

[3] T. C. Helvey, *The Age of Information: An Interdisciplinary Survey of Cybernetics* (Englewood Cliffs, N.J.: Educational Technology Publications, 1971), p. 7.

[4] Rudy Bretz, *A Taxonomy of Communication Media* (Englewood Cliffs, N.J.: Educational Technology Publications, 1971), pp. 11-16.

a user. Some question the degree to which practitioners in the field can or should translate theory into action, the argument being that knowing the communication process from a theoretical standpoint does not insure the production of a quality, purposeful message. Nevertheless, one must assume that knowing about the communication process may help media specialists answer information requests and assist them in producing better communications.

In a learning procedure a media specialist might be working with a student who wants to know something about plant and animal cells. Since all kinds of materials about cells exist on many levels, it would be rather poor procedure to encourage the student to look up cells in the card catalog or to give him a general science textbook or reference book. A better first step would be to ask the student his particular interest in cells. To keep the example simple, suppose that he simply needs to learn the basic parts of a generalized plant cell and a generalized animal cell. At this point the media specialist must know what best communicates parts of things—what materials match the learning requirements of the task. In this case, pictures and diagrams would seem to be appropriate. The second thing the media specialist must know is that memorization is the learning dimension. Consequently, the student needs something to study, something to glance at whenever he wants, until he masters the basic parts of cells. A fifteen-minute film comparing plant and animal cells is not likely to do this specific job because the input is not explicit enough or present long enough for learning to take place. Encouragement to explore, to know more than the parts of a generalized cell, and to appreciate cellular structure in living things is more likely to be received favorably after the student's specific need is satisfied.

Media personnel are concerned with the total communication process. The media program includes the relationships established between elements (student, media specialist, and materials) as well as the elements themselves. The concept that school media specialists can or even should be communication experts is naive; however, it is equally naive to expect a media specialist to recommend what messages should be transmitted orally, visually, pictorially, physically, or in a particular multimedia format unless he has a functional understanding of the nature of information as it relates to the communication process.

### INFORMATION AND ACCULTURATION

A central purpose of the schools is to provide experiences within a framework which will enable students to gain and use information, to adjust, and to find ways to contribute. Herein lies one of the basic conflicts between what the school is doing and what the student feels he needs. If a basic tenet is that all students strive to adjust and to contribute, then goals of adjustment and contribution must be ascertained. Early in every child's life he begins to sort out "school" experiences from "real" experiences. The gap appears most prominently in rural, ghetto, and central city schools where the socio-economic condition of the student is in conflict with the middle-class value system on which the school curriculum rests. In many instances, the problem of whose culture shall be transmitted blocks the development of content and experience which transcend cultural patterns. In these cases the schools continually manifest assumptions discontinuous with those of the immediate cultural context. Media can help bridge this gap and can make learning more immediate, productive, and individual.[5]

Films, stories, records, and many other media have the unique ability to extend experience—to literally bring the world into the classroom as well as provide for vicarious experience. Such forms of media as programmed texts and auto-tutorial laboratories make learning more productive and more individualized. Media are successful with large audiences as well as with individuals seeking to extend their understanding and appreciation of themselves and their world. In this context, the schools and society are what their information bases allow them to be.

Educating individuals to make positive and unique contributions to society has to be a vital part of the school curriculum. The implication is that anyone may do or be anything he can as long as he does not infringe upon the freedom of others. This view, in turn, imposes criteria on the kind of education suitable. For example, educational institutions must help individuals overcome blocks to effective, self-rewarding citizenship. Schools must provide equal opportunity for the development of self. In effect, schools must be a microcosm of what society wants to become.

Many attempts have been made to identify what society expects of its schools. Possibly the great failure of the schools has been their inability to develop ways and means to translate the goals set by the general culture into educational programs that relate to the many subcultures that make up society. The kind and type of information a media center provides must communicate to the specific publics served.

As early as 1918, with the publication of the *Cardinal Principles of Secondary Education,* an attempt was made to provide goals for schools. This study by the Commission on the Reorganization of Secondary Edu-

---

[5] Sidney G. Tickton, ed., *To Improve Learning: An Evaluation of Instructional Technology,* Vol. I (New York: Bowker, 1970), p. 10.

cation emphasized seven goals of education: (1) health, (2) command of fundamental processes, (3) worthy home membership, (4) vocation, (5) citizenship, (6) worthy use of leisure time, and (7) ethical character.[6]

The Educational Policies Commission of the National Education Association (NEA) challenged the schools in 1944 to relate their programs to the ten imperative needs of all youth. The commission urged schools to build programs which provided opportunities for youth to (1) acquire salable skills; (2) develop good health; (3) understand and fulfill obligations to the community, state, nation, and world; (4) understand and appreciate successful family life; (5) become wise consumers; (6) understand methods and influences of science on human life; (7) appreciate literature, art, music, and nature; (8) use leisure time wisely; (9) develop respect, cooperation, and ethical behavior; and (10) think rationally, communicate effectively, and read and listen with understanding.[7]

More recently the Harvard Report (1945), the Rockefeller Report (1958), and the Report of the United States Commission on National Goals (1960) have stressed the need to prepare youth for participation in a democracy by providing experiences which facilitate individual growth.[8] Each report underscored the necessity for a type of liberal education as prerequisite for full citizenship. The Harvard Report stressed the need to produce educational programs which develop an appreciation for the benefits, privileges, and responsibilities of citizens in a free, democratic society. The report recognized that schools must provide a wide variety of opportunities. Equality in education was not envisioned as an identical education for all. Rather, the concept of equality in education was developed to provide for individual differences.

Both the Rockefeller Report and the President's Commission on National Goals stressed the dependent relationship between (1) the quality of educational opportunities and (2) the power and potential of society. Both reports charged that current educational programs were mediocre and impersonal and that provisions should be made for a diversity of

---

[6] NEA Commission on the Reorganization of Secondary Education, *Cardinal Principles of Secondary Education,* U.S. Bureau of Education Bulletin No. 35 (Washington, D.C.: Govt. Print. Off., 1918).

[7] NEA Educational Policies Commission, *Education for ALL American Youth* (Washington, D.C.: the Association, 1944).

[8] Harvard Committee, *General Education in a Free Society* (Cambridge: Harvard Univ. Pr., 1945); *The Pursuit of Excellence: Education and the Future of America* (New York: Doubleday, 1958); President's Commission on National Goals, *Goals for Americans* (Englewood Cliffs, N.J.: Prentice-Hall, 1960).

experiences designed to nurture respect for each individual. The President's Commission on National Goals stressed the need to create educational programs that support the rights of individuals. The commission both encouraged the development of new teaching techniques in order to strengthen education at all levels and in every discipline and repeatedly emphasized that education and citizenship must be taken more seriously by all Americans.

The Center for the Study of Evaluation at the University of California reported in 1972 on the collective viewpoints of 2,555 people—principals (192), teachers (1,184), and parents (1,179)—throughout the United States. Participants were requested to sort 106 goals into 5 categories entitled (1) unimportant, irrelevant, (2) marginal importance, (3) average importance, (4) moderate importance, or (5) most important. These goals were identified from sources including curriculum guides, textbooks, and studies of various kinds. Although all goals might contribute to self-actualization and acculturation, the top six selected were directly related. Of these six, self-esteem, need achievement, and neuroticism-adjustment directly related to the development of self-actualized students, while citizenship, socialization-rebelliousness, and school orientation focused on goals leading to acculturation.[9]

Educational literature abounds with translations, elaborations, and applications of goals stressing self-actualization and acculturation. However, it is most distressing that while leaders in society have continued to stress these goals, the gap between society's expectations of schools and what schools deliver continues to grow. In a general response to what the schools *are* doing, the Community National Field Task Force on the Improvement and Reform of American Education states:

> The community has been the last hired, first fired, last consulted, first insulted, last informed and first blamed—every effort has been made to drive them away. . . . Time and time again, elements of this group have been faked out and victimized by false promises, fake panaceas, and paper programs. They have had huge sums siphoned off in their name by universities and school system overlords.
>
> The Task Force believes that no change or improvement is possible in public education without actually involving the consumer in the change process—the student, his family, and the adults of the neighborhood (the local taxpayers). The consumer must be involved not merely in the *choice* of alternatives, but also in the determination and the clarification of goals

---

[9] Center for the Study of Evaluation, *A Guidebook for CSE Elementary School Evaluation Kit* (Boston: Allyn and Bacon, 1972), pp. 9-10, 16, 24-25.

and objectives, and in the monitoring and evaluating of the processes and procedures, as well as in the implementing of the program.[10]

This seeming indifference of the schools to the task must end. To develop the process by which the needs of society can be analyzed and satisfied through effective educational programs is *the* responsibility of educators at all levels.

The complexity of this task increases at an alarming rate. As society becomes more complex, so does the task of educating youth. As the technology shifts, segments of the educational enterprise become obsolete. As specialization increases, parts of society become isolated, producing misunderstandings and indifference. When the mythology of the culture is replaced with demonstrable knowledge, segments of the culture lose orientation. The number of needed changes increases while the amount of time available to initiate needed changes decreases.

The task of helping each child find, evaluate, utilize, and generate the information needed to become a self-actualized, acculturated individual is complicated by the rapidly expanding information base of the culture. Information doubles every eight years, pouring from practically every human activity. Children view more than eight thousand hours of television during their preschool years, thereby entering school with a technological sophistication that often exceeds the school's capacity to respond. Mass media keep learners instantly informed and often frustrated by articulating problems which seem strangely isolated from school programs. In addition, mass media make the problems of the world community evident to the young, who must reconcile the myopic behavior of the culture with the needs of people everywhere if they are to free themselves to engage in more abstract learning activities.

The rate of change being experienced by society is in direct proportion to the expanding information base upon which society is built. Information of importance to society must shape educational goals. Being able to communicate and to find the information needed is the essence of cohesion in the social system. In order to discover how decisions are being made within society, one must study the communication networks. Organizational charts rarely disclose who is talking to whom, where the decision makers are getting their information, and who is better able to find the information and to articulate his point. As society continues to

[10] Community National Field Task Force on the Improvement and Reform of American Education, *A Real Alternative: The Final Report and Recommendations of the Community National Field Task Force on the Improvement and Reform of American Education,* Publication No. OE-74-12007 (Washington, D.C.: Dept. of Health, Education, and Welfare, 1974), p. 54.

change, the quantity and quality of information available to learners will determine whether or not they even have a chance to adjust, to process the input, to realize their potential, and to become self-actualized individuals.

## INFORMATION AND SELF-ACTUALIZATION

Day-by-day routines, goals, judgments, and willingness to change are dependent upon an individual's view of self in society which includes a perception of individual purposes and capacities.[11] The cautious manner in which many school media specialists approach change reflects perceptions of the purposes and capacities of themselves as well as others. Media specialists who believe they can contribute to the curriculum building process and who believe teachers want and need their help will function on these fronts. Perceptions of what students can do and should do determine what they are allowed to do. Individuals with limited perceptions not only build invisible walls around themselves but also restrict the activities of others.

In a sense, there is a kind of psychological inertia which contributes to characterization of self. If an individual believes he is able, he continues to develop that picture; if he believes he is incapable, he strives just as hard to enhance that picture.[12] Considerable energy is frequently necessary to change direction or pace. The environment of the individual nurtures or restricts, facilitates or discourages change; the environment provides the sensory input, the information that is processed by the individual. Consequently, the psychological, physiological, social, and intellectual status of an individual reflects the information received from his environment.

## INFORMATION SOURCES

The real world and its artifacts as well as pictorial, symbolic, verbal, and multiform media provide the information and experience base on which the culture is built. As learners interact with the world, they process sensory input which develops a unique view of the universe. Media extend the senses, one's perception, and total sensorium.[13] The

[11] Association for Supervision and Curriculum Development, *Perceiving, Behaving, Becoming* (Washington, D.C.: Assn. for Supervision and Curriculum Development, National Education Assn., 1962), p. 1.

[12] Muriel Beadle, *A Child's Mind* (Garden City, N.Y.: Doubleday, 1970), p. 264.

[13] Hayden R. Smith, "Media Men Arise: What If McLuhan Is Right?" *Educational Screen and Audiovisual Guide* 47:18-19 (June 1968).

media specialist's task is to manage and to promote appropriate use of all media. There is no basic competition among media as sources of information. The book–nonbook dichotomy makes little sense to a media specialist. Declaring, "I am a book person," or holding up a book and saying, "You are looking at a relic of an obsolete technology," suggests concern for the package and not the content. To improve the teaching-learning process, the emphasis must be on what learners can gain from using all media. Media specialists, therefore, are concerned with the advantages and disadvantages of media as ways to learn.

Each form of media provides a unique experience and as such stands as a metaphor suggesting a likeness or analogy between objects and ideas.[14] Since media are metaphors, they inevitably stress and suppress what they represent. Hence, each has its particular purposes, strengths, and weaknesses. Translating information from one form or package to another involves adding, summarizing, reducing, clarifying, and some-times even obscuring the original content. Translations also require an understanding of the encoding forms—language, symbols, pictures, mod-els—utilized by a specific media or media-mix.

Familiar media frequently employ a mixture of such encoding forms as language, symbols, and pictures. Media, such as programs of instruction, may use forms within forms—audio tapes, filmstrips, and records. As a consequence, many films, books, filmstrips, transparencies, and programs of instruction may also be considered multimedia. One of the principal values in considering media in terms of the types of encoding forms employed is that once the encoders are known, identifying strengths and weaknesses in the communication is facilitated. The consideration here is the way encoders form metaphors. Effect depends on how media con-dense or expand reality, eliminate distractions, speed up or slow down information output, and reduce the cost of information transmission.[15]

Creative communication demands both freedom and constraint. Free-dom must be exercised in order to investigate, experiment with, and combine materials and communication (presentation) forms in new and original ways. Constraint must be practiced in order to recognize and evaluate strengths and limitations (capacities) of materials and presenta-tion forms. Learning to utilize the unique characteristics of all forms requires continuous experiences. The potential for creatively responding

---

[14] Marshall McLuhan, *Understanding Media* (New York: McGraw-Hill, 1964), p. 57.

[15] Donald T. Tosti and John R. Ball, *A Behavioral Approach to Instructional De-sign and Media Selection* (Albuquerque: Behavior Systems Division, Westinghouse Learning Corp., 1969), p. 25.

increases as the components—time, personnel, facilities, materials, and equipment—are expanded.

Communicating well through media demands a high degree of comprehension of the subject to be communicated and consequently constitutes a high-level educational activity. For example, when students are designing a communication, they should drop the unimportant, stress the main concepts, and provide appropriate illustrations. Ever since education has been viewed in experimental terms students have been encouraged to become involved. Involvement increases the intensity, fidelity, and accuracy derived by information users. Higher degrees of frustration, satisfaction, and excitement are felt by those who are creating than by those who are only passively receiving information. In order to know the capacities and limitations of media, students and teachers must be able to touch, manipulate, and experiment.

Learning by creating media should be distinguished from the popular concept of multimedia experience. A long-held belief is that the greater the sensory involvement the greater the possibility that learning will take place. Ultimately, this conviction could lead to a kind of total sensory immersion which is in conflict with the reason for developing encoding forms and using them in specific ways. The purpose of employing a particular encoding form is to condense, to speed up information output, and to reduce the cost of transmission. For example, graphing information from a chapter discussing population growth trends can quickly transmit selected aspects of the chapter. The number and kind of media employed must be determined through an analysis of the mission. Generally speaking, developing a total impression, creating an attitude, or stimulating creative endeavors may be encouraged by a meaningful, artistic collage of encoding forms. The more specific the learning required, the more specifically the encoding form may be identified.

Increasing the contact of students with information sources means providing a greater variety of media as well as the opportunity to communicate through many presentation forms. Media should not be viewed as competing forms but rather as complementary systems. Maximum mileage can be achieved from information sources by involving students in the process of selecting, utilizing, experimenting, and producing as well as evaluating. The purpose of increased involvement is to help students grow as individuals (self-actualization) and contribute to society (acculturation) in a mutually rewarding manner.

### Implications for the Media Program

1. The goals of society are translated into educational programs (modes of inquiry) which, in turn, set the parameters of the media program. Studies have repeatedly emphasized acculturation and self-actualization as the central concerns of educational programs.

2. The media program applies principles of best educational practice and techniques for developing more technologically responsible systems. The media center provides through its materials and programs the ways and means to view the world objectively and to investigate the nature of man.

3. The processes of gathering, evaluating, utilizing, and generating information constitute a substantial part of any educational program. Each of these processes provides opportunity for media program development.

4. The human brain utilizes information in order to form perceptions of the world as well as attitudes toward those perceptions. Consequently, the greater the number, quality, and variety of resources utilized in the educational program, the richer the educational experience. Media help bridge differences among cultures and individuals and can make learning more immediate, productive, and individual.

5. Understanding media means being able to utilize, to translate, and to evaluate encoding forms. Communication models such as the one developed by Shannon and Weaver isolate elements and show interrelationships, providing media specialists a language for discussing what and why phenomena occur during a communication.

6. Evaluation of media is made in terms of learner (user) needs. Media provide alternative ways to meet curricular objectives. The media center organizes resources in many formats and on many levels in order to respond to the varied and specific needs of users.

7. Media specialists provide leadership and consultative services related to the process of instructional design. This process involves students and teachers in producing, utilizing, evaluating, and repackaging of learning materials.

8. All aspects of the media program encourage students and teachers to explore new materials and to expand their ability to utilize learning resources creatively.

## Problems and Activities for Research and Discussion

1. What obstacles do schools encounter in the process of building curricula developed from goals identified by agencies such as the Educational Policies Commission of NEA? Why is the development of programs that relate to the concerns of society a moral as well as a professional obligation?

2. Why may information, literally and figuratively, be considered "the energy that enables society to perpetuate itself and to transcend that which is"?

3. Why should media specialists be concerned with defining terms such as *information, knowledge,* and *instruction?*

4. What constitutes "useful" information?

5. Why should media specialists be concerned with the impact of mass media on learners?

6. Develop a classification scheme for media, using encoding forms.

7. Isolate and discuss characteristics of a self-actualized individual.

8. Defend or refute: The real value of the media program is in its ability to transcend the educational program of a school.

9. Defend or refute: Society has demonstrated an unbelievable degree of unconcern for the educational enterprise.

## Sample Minimodule

### Relationships between Modes of Inquiry and Information Resources

PROBLEM. Media professionals have long recognized the importance of participating in the curriculum planning process. If they are to help implement the curriculum of the school, the *why* seems obvious. *How* media professionals are to participate seems less well defined. One positive contribution media professionals can make relates to identifying information resources which match modes of inquiry or teaching and learning strategies. In other words, if the objectives, content, and teaching-learning techniques are known, the appropriateness of various information resources becomes clearer.

PERFORMANCE OBJECTIVES.

1. Using the book *Models of Teaching* by Bruce Joyce and Marsha Weil (Englewood Cliffs, N.J., Prentice-Hall, Inc., 1972), the student will

list the primary information source and three secondary information sources for each mode of inquiry and write a description of the method used to process the information identified (see chart).

| OBJECTIVE | MODEL | PRIMARY INFORMATION SOURCES | SECONDARY INFORMATION SOURCES | WAYS OF PROCESSING INFORMATION* |
|---|---|---|---|---|
| The student will list 5 advantages and 5 disadvantages of the democratic process. | Democratic Process (Thelen) | . . . . . . . . . . | . . . . . . . . . . . . . . . . . . . . . . | . . . . . . . . . . . . . . . . . . . . . . . . . . . . . . . . . . . . . . |
| | Concept Attainment (Bruner) | . . . . . . . . . . | . . . . . . . . . . . . . . . . . . . . . . | . . . . . . . . . . . . . . . . . . . . . . . . . . . . . . . . . . . . . . |
| | Classroom Meeting (Glasser) | . . . . . . . . . . | . . . . . . . . . . . . . . . . . . . . . . | . . . . . . . . . . . . . . . . . . . . . . . . . . . . . . . . . . . . . . |
| The student will prepare a poster illustrating one source of environmental pollution. | Social Inquiry (Massialas and Cox) | . . . . . . . . . . | . . . . . . . . . . . . . . . . . . . . . . | . . . . . . . . . . . . . . . . . . . . . . . . . . . . . . . . |
| | Expository Teaching (Ausubel) | . . . . . . . . . . | . . . . . . . . . . . . . . . . . . . . . . | . . . . . . . . . . . . . . . . . . . . . . . . . . . . . . . . . . . . . . |
| | Synectics (Gordon) | . . . . . . . . . . | . . . . . . . . . . . . . . . . . . . . . . | . . . . . . . . . . . . . . . . . . . . . . . . . . . . . . . . . . . . . . |
| The student will make 100 ml of oxygen. | Democratic Process (Thelen) | . . . . . . . . . . | . . . . . . . . . . . . . . . . . . . . . . | . . . . . . . . . . . . . . . . . . . . . . . . . . . . . . . . . . . . . . |
| | Inductive Model (Taba) | . . . . . . . . . . | . . . . . . . . . . . . . . . . . . . . . . | . . . . . . . . . . . . . . . . . . . . . . . . . . . . . . . . . . . . . . |
| | Non-Directive Teaching (Rogers) | . . . . . . . . . . | . . . . . . . . . . . . . . . . . . . . . . | . . . . . . . . . . . . . . . . . . . . . . . . . . . . . . . . . . . . . . |

*For example, descriptions of methods may be one of the following: group interaction and consensus; inductive or deductive reasoning; content summaries; translation of information from one format to another; applying information to the production; producing experimental data.

2. Given the information collected on the chart, the student will select the most appropriate model for each objective and write a paragraph in defense of each selection.

3. The student will match each mode identified on the chart to (a) a descriptive statement of each mode, (b) the principal developer of each mode (cited on the chart), and (c) the primary information source for each mode.

SUGGESTIONS FOR DEVELOPING CRITERION MEASURE. The following examples may be applied to *each* performance objective in order appearing under PERFORMANCE OBJECTIVES.

1. Is the chart complete, accurate, specific, and clearly presented?

2. Is the selection appropriate? Is the defense congruent with the concepts presented by Joyce and Weil?

3. (a)  Match.

        _____ Synectics   A.  Structure of the discipline
                               B.  Creative exploration
                               C.  Nondirective counseling
                               D.  Inductive learning

(b)  Massialas and Cox developed the mode identified as
        _____ A.  Expository teaching
        _____ B.  Democratic process
        _____ C.  Concept attainment
        _____ D.  Social inquiry

(c)  The primary information source for nondirective teaching is
        _____ A.  All literature
        _____ B.  Single discipline centered
        _____ C.  Self
        _____ D.  The teacher

REFERENCES

Association for Supervision and Curriculum Development. *Perceiving, Behaving, Becoming.* Washington, D.C.: The Association, 1962.

Beadle, Muriel. *A Child's Mind.* Garden City, N.Y.: Doubleday, 1970.

Belson, William A. *The Impact of Television.* Hamden, Conn.: Archon, 1967.

Berlo, David K. *The Process of Communication.* New York: Holt, Rinehart, and Winston, 1960.

Bretz, Rudy. *A Taxonomy of Communication Media.* Englewood Cliffs, N.J.: Educational Technology Publications, 1971.

Center for the Study of Evaluation. *A Guidebook for CSE Elementary School Evaluation Kit.* Boston: Allyn and Bacon, 1972.

Community National Field Task Force on the Improvement and Reform of American Education. *A Real Alternative: The Final Report and Recommendations of the Community National Field Task Force on the Improvement and Reform of American Education.* Publication No. OE-74-12007. Washington, D.C.: Department of Health, Education and Welfare, 1974.

Davies, Ruth Ann. *The School Library: A Force for Educational Excellence.* 2nd ed. New York: Bowker, 1974.

Erickson, Carlton W. H. *Administering Instructional Media Programs.* New York: Macmillan, 1968.

Gattegno, Caleb. *Towards a Visual Culture.* New York: Outerbridge and Dienstfrey, 1969.

Gerlach, Vernon S., and Ely, Donald P. *Teaching and Media: A Systematic Approach.* Englewood Cliffs, N.J.: Prentice-Hall, 1971.

Harvard Committee. *General Education in a Free Society.* Cambridge: Harvard Univ. Pr., 1945.

Helvey, T. C. *The Age of Information: An Interdisciplinary Survey of Cybernetics.* Englewood Cliffs, N.J.: Educational Technology Publications, 1971.

Hug, William E., ed. *Strategies for Change in Information Programs.* New York: Bowker, 1974.

Joyce, Bruce, and Weil, Marsha. *Models of Teaching.* Englewood Cliffs, N.J.: Prentice-Hall, 1972.

McLuhan, Marshall. *Understanding Media.* New York: McGraw-Hill, 1964.

NEA Commission on the Reorganization of Secondary Education. *Cardinal Principles of Secondary Education.* U.S. Bureau of Education Bulletin No. 35. Washington, D.C.: Govt. Print. Off., 1918.

NEA Educational Policies Commission. *Education for ALL American Youth.* Washington, D.C.: National Education Association, 1944.

President's Commission on National Goals. *Goals for Americans.* Englewood Cliffs, N.J.: Prentice-Hall, 1960.

*The Pursuit of Excellence: Education and the Future of America.* New York: Doubleday, 1958.

Sereno, Kenneth K. *Foundations of Communication Theory.* New York: Harper and Row, 1970.

Shannon, Claude, and Weaver, Warren. *The Mathematical Theory of Communication.* Urbana: Univ. of Illinois Pr., 1949.

Smith, Alfred G. *Communication and Culture.* New York: Holt, Rinehart and Winston, 1966.

Smith, Hayden R. "Media Men Arise: What If McLuhan Is Right?" *Educational Screen and Audiovisual Guide* 47:18-19 (June 1968).

Steinberg, Charles S. *Mass Media and Communication.* New York: Hastings House, 1966.

Tickton, Sidney G., ed. *To Improve Learning: An Evaluation of Instructional Technology.* 2 vols. New York: Bowker, 1970.

Tosti, Donald T., and Ball, John R. *A Behavioral Approach to Instructional Design and Media Selection.* Albuquerque: Behavior Systems Division, Westinghouse Learning Corp., 1969.

Travers, Robert M. W. *Man's Information System: A Primer for Media Specialists and Educational Technologists.* Scranton: Chandler, 1970.

Trump, J. Lloyd, and Miller, Delmas F. *Secondary School Curriculum Improvement.* Boston: Allyn and Bacon, 1968.

Vickery, B. C. *On Retrieval System Theory.* Hamden, Conn.: Archon, 1965.

# General Curriculum Movements

THROUGHOUT THE history of education its thrust has been influenced by broad theoretical responses to the times. Even though the purposes change from era to era, the proven techniques or modes of inquiry utilized for attaining purposes seem to endure. For example, during the Greek classical period the purpose of Spartan education was to prepare citizens to labor, to fight, and to conquer; Athenian education preserved the family and placed emphasis on reading, writing, and literary elements of education.[1] During that time the Socratic method, a technique of inductive reasoning through conversation, was developed. Today, this basic technique is considered a viable mode of inquiry for teaching and learning many concepts. Likewise, the techniques of formal logic and the scientific method have provided modes that remain even though purposes may change.

Regardless of the emphasis of movements, modes of inquiry are interchangeable. The learner may use problem-solving, inquiry, sensitivity training, programmed materials, or a combination of these. Some curricula may tend to give more credibility to one method over others; nevertheless, all past curricular movements could have found a place for most modes of inquiry currently popular.

The degree that best educational practice and technological responsibility exists in each curriculum movement seems to be independent from

---

[1] Francesco Cordasco, *A Brief History of Education* (Paterson, N.J.: Littlefield, Adams, 1963), p. 5.

21

the movement itself. For example, the proponents of the subject-organized curriculum support the theory that the primary source of educational objectives are the disciplines themselves. On the other hand, supporters of the social processes curriculum believe that the primary source of educational objectives comes from the values and needs of the social order. These two points of view reflect different philosophical positions which are independent from the modes of inquiry an individual classroom teacher may or may not be employing.

Whether or not a field of general curriculum theory and development exists is debatable. Traditionally, the area of curriculum attempts to (1) describe various broad movements in terms of the social, philosophical, and psychological principles that support them; (2) outline a procedure for curriculum planning, development, and decision-making; and (3) describe trends in various subject areas. In addition, curriculum workers and schools of education often take a bandwagon approach, embracing the popular movement and excluding all others. For example, during the years universities and school systems encouraged development of core curricula, they discouraged discipline-centered programs. Today, humanistic, competency-based, and career education movements enjoy the same support core curricula once did. Many are arguing that sociological, philosophical, and psychological foundations provide the base for curriculum study. Some view the base as systems theory, instructional technology, or subject areas. Moreover, others suggest that the field of general curriculum is simply a synthesis of all of these.

PROBLEMS OF GENERAL CURRICULUM THEORY AND DEVELOPMENT

The discomforts of those involved in curriculum theory and development are numerous. First, a view of the curriculum as all the planned and incidental experiences a child has during his presence at school creates an unmanageable concept. As a solution, Foshay separates the formal educational program from acculturation and self-actualization as he defines three levels of the curriculum:

Curriculum I is the formal academic offering, plus those cocurricular activities that are planned. It consists in the main of school subjects, occasionally organized on a broad fields basis, more frequently organized around the disciplines they represent.

Curriculum II, sometimes called the "latent" curriculum, has to do with the nature and function of authority in life, the problems of participation in the decisions that make one's own life, and in general with social development.

Curriculum III is a curriculum in self-awareness and in self development. If curriculum II deals mainly with the social aspects of what it means to be a human being, curriculum III deals mainly with the private aspects of what it means to be human.[2]

Tying down the curriculum in this manner seems more manageable, especially if curriculum I is viewed as a vehicle for developing curricula II and III. Nevertheless, no one worker or group of workers has the knowledge or theoretical basis to interpret all of an individual's experiences in each of these three curricula. Accountablity, justifying the means to the ends, then becomes a frustrating consideration and is beyond what can reasonably be expected of a classroom teacher. In other words, the teacher is programmed for incompetence. This is probably one reason why the concept of the curriculum as all the schoolhouse experiences of the child is ignored by most teachers as they face the constant task of *What Do I Do Monday?*[3]

The second problem pushes deeper than discomfort as the credibility of various groups becomes suspect. University professors and, to a great extent, directors of curriculum are concerned with accounting for the whole in a more or less descriptive sense. This seems to leave the teacher who needs help most and who may lack an understanding of both content and process, to survive somehow without the help of these so-called experts. In some instances subject matter supervisors and consultants have helped bridge this gap. However, the subject supervisor is frequently spread too thin, is not available when needed, or is unable to provide the specific expertise for the immediate task. After all, what can one reasonably expect of a curriculum director concerned with all the experiences boys and girls have during school hours or a subject supervisor who is responsible for language arts for kindergarten through the twelfth grade?

In a very real sense, the survival of each group—university professors, curriculum directors, subject supervisors, and elementary and secondary teachers—depends upon the ability to solve different kinds of problems developed from different concerns which reflect different, and sometimes conflicting, purposes. Suspicion and antagonism naturally develop as the teacher finds that the supervisor is of little help in solving immediate problems; as the district director attempts to politically respond to the pressures of subject supervisors in relation to the restrictions imposed by the superintendent; and as both groups sit through a summer's graduate course in curriculum development where the professor spends long hours

---

[2] Arthur W. Foshay, *Curriculum for the 70's: An Agenda for Invention* (Washington, D.C.: National Education Association, 1970), pp. 28-32.

[3] John Holt, *What Do I Do Monday?* (New York: Dutton, 1970).

talking about personal perceptions of the sociological, philosophical, and psychological forces that impinge on life in general and incidentally on the curriculum.

The third discomforting set of experiences involves the processes by which curricula are developed. All concerned seem to be demanding the freedom to do what they want to do, at the same time seeking to find justification in terms of the whole. As a consequence one could argue that the less professors of curriculum development know about the classroom the happier they may be. The same can be said, to some extent, about each group.

The processes of assembling committees to vote on the acceptance or rejection of courses, forming national committees to restructure content areas, bringing teachers in for summers to prepare curriculum guides, and selecting textbooks all affect one another yet are strangely isolated. One may argue that in many cases voting simply replaces knowing whether or not a course or set of experiences is needed. Whether determining curriculum or sexing gerbils, if one does not know what to look for, one can always vote on it and perhaps be right at least 50 percent of the time. In *The Real World of the Public Schools,* Harry S. Broudy criticizes development of curricula through committees of so-called representative groups:

> This process of constructing curricula by consensus is a bow in the direction of democracy, a bow that becomes a full-fledged genuflection when the total citizenry is invited to participate. Neither the teachers nor the citizens participate because of their special knowledge about what needs to be taught.[4]

This widespread criticism of making curriculum decisions via committee action invariably relates to the way members are selected as well as to the lack of operational guidelines for committees which include specified tasks and responsibilities. Members are too frequently selected for political reasons and not because they possess a specific competency needed for the committee to complete its charge. Politically oriented members plus separate committees, operating independently as they designate new courses, select textbooks, and prepare curriculum guides, encourage arbitrary administrative decisions in order to move forward with some kind of unified program. In other words, the process by which curricula emerge is rarely thought out in any functional sense and may block program development.

---

[4] Harry S. Broudy, *The Real World of the Public Schools* (New York: Harcourt Brace Jovanovich, 1972), pp. 41-42.

National movements to restructure content areas have greatly contributed to the development and updating of content areas but have almost universally ignored priorities established by the work of such organizations as NEA Commission on the Reorganization of Secondary Education, NEA Educational Policies Commission, the Harvard Committee, and the President's Commission on National Goals. Summer workshops tend to produce outlines which are confined to selected textbooks, feasible activities, and resources locally available. Conversation may be concerned with what should be done, but action is constantly tied to what can be done.

The fourth frustrating factor again relates to what is rather than to what should be. In an abstract but at the same time realistic sense, the curriculum is like a liquid; it flows in all directions and occupies all of the space regardless of the size or shape of the container. Consequently, the length of a class period, the flexibility of the schedule, the skills of the teacher, the media collection, the presence or absence of window shades, the location of the principal's office, and the size of the gym are all conditions that affect what shape the curriculum may take. What can be done is done. What should be done is left for tomorrow.

The fifth discomforting situation arises through continuous reorganization. Administrators are constantly reminded that they are in charge and are responsible for curriculum leadership within their schools and districts. Consequently, they respond as they can; they reorganize. Kettering Foundation's Individually Guided Education is a classic example of an attempt to administratively change the decision-making process so that more individualized programs can evolve. Team teaching, flexible scheduling, combining and creating departments, combining and creating and eliminating positions are all employed in an effort to change the curriculum. The history of American education seems to be a series of organizational changes produced to accommodate an idea that has not been adequately—at least not functionally—defined or justified.

The Core curriculum movement was quite diffused and therefore difficult to define, a point usually commented on by writers on the subject. However, most Core programs seemed to have been characterized by 'learning activities' that were regarded as basic for all students; that cut across conventional subject matter lines, either 'fusing' or disregarding them entirely; that used a relatively large block of time (some Core classes were called 'blocktime classes'); that provided for extensive teacher-pupil planning; and that were strongly oriented to student 'needs, problems, and interests.'[5]

[5] Hazel W. Hertzberg, *Historical Parallels for the Sixties and Seventies: Primary Sources and Core Curriculum Revisited* (ERIC Microfiche, ED 51-066), p. 13.

The sixth condition which leaves everyone stranded from time to time is the school's colossal inability to give alternatives a fair trial. Shifts are made from thematical approaches to linguistic approaches, from workbooks to textbooks, from large content areas to mini-courses, from descriptive biology to process biology and on and on. Does each change represent progress? No one seems to know for sure.

The seventh factor contributing to discomfort is the degree to which commercial houses are producing the curriculum for the schools. Adoption of some programs of instruction make teachers feel they are functioning in less than a professional role, or that they are too confined to the step-by-step procedures demanded by a particular system. Control over the utilization of large commercial programs is largely in the hands of teachers who select and change programs at will. No one knows for sure if the integrity of the program is being violated or if the concepts the program is designed to teach become lost when changes are made. Lecture-oriented physics teachers cannot develop the inductive reasoning skills that PSSC Physics (Physical Science Study Commission) demand unless they are willing to stop what they are doing and start functioning as directors of laboratory activities. In other words, the production and implementation of large, well-organized instructional programs prescribe the role of the teacher and the student to a degree that is in conflict with the more or less free agent concept of the classroom teacher. To put it another way, as better programs become available (better meaning *valid*), the role of students and teachers will be more prescriptive. Since the best teachers currently in the schools may be there simply because teaching allows them to function in a free and creative way, there is a fear that large commercial blocks of instruction will discourage the development of this most valuable kind of professional.

As the curriculum contracts or expands to meet the constraints imposed, people occupying key positions tend to create their own independent systems and strive for autonomy and meaning. Each discomforting factor discussed represents a kind of independent system frequently existing for one purpose and operating in order to achieve personal purposes more related to survival than to cause. In a sense, each contributes to the other; in another sense, each is blocking the development of the other because the two frequently exist at cross purposes.

### SUBJECT-ORGANIZED CURRICULUM

Over the years the credibility of curricula organized around discrete subject areas has seemingly weathered most storms. This is so for a number of reasons, but first and foremost the subject-organized school program is the easiest to conceptualize and to implement. This is not to say that subjects themselves do not change. As man's information base grows, so does the number of specialities or subject areas. Although the proliferation of subject areas is most noticeable on the collegiate level, the impact can also be seen in secondary and elementary schools. For example, there is an increased interest in subjects such as economics, ecology, anthropology, and career training at all levels. In the subject-organized school program, curriculum genesis and renewal usually takes the form of accommodating new knowledge into the curriculum.

Modern defenders of curricula that are organized around discrete subjects point to the need for people to be able to apply modes of inquiry unique to each subject area. Broudy, Smith, and Burnett have attempted to integrate man's knowledge into five new subject areas:

1. symbolics of information—language and mathematics
2. basic sciences
3. developmental studies—evolution of the cosmos, evolution of social institutions, and evolution of man's culture
4. exemplars—art, music, drama, literature
5. molar problems—typical social problems.[6]

Regardless of the specific subjects advocated, most supporters of subject-organized curricula believe that content should be derived from the fields of disciplined inquiry, should be representative of the field as a whole, should exemplify methods of inquiry and modes of understanding, and should be selected to promote understanding and to arouse enthusiasm and imagination.[7]

### SOCIAL PROCESSES CURRICULUM

Curricula based on social processes attempt to relate the school's formal program to life. Curricula based on social processes and life functions are attempts to integrate discrete content areas into patterns which will respond more directly to questions such as:

1. who am I?
2. what makes me human?
3. how can I stay healthy?
4. what kind of work am I suited for?
5. why morality?

[6] Harry S. Broudy, B. Othanel Smith, and Joe R. Burnett, *Democracy and Excellence in Secondary Education* (Chicago: Rand McNally, 1964), p. 78.
[7] Philip H. Phenix, "The Architectonics of Knowledge," in *Education and the Structure of Knowledge,* ed. Stanley Elam (Chicago: Rand McNally, 1964), pp. 44-74.

Building a curriculum around questions such as these is an attempt to show that information can be used to help man solve personal and immediate problems. Such curricula purport to give meaning to the school by utilizing the experiential background of the learners, by analyzing principles which relate to all cultures, and by providing a standard for choosing content.

In 1937, Frederick and Farquear suggested nine topics to be used as a basis for curriculum organization:

1. protecting life and health
2. getting a living
3. making a home
4. expressing religious impulses
5. satisfying the desire for beauty
6. securing education
7. cooperating in social and civic action
8. engaging in recreation
9. improving material conditions.[8]

School programs that are built around topics such as these require a much different collection of resources than a school organized around discrete subject areas. In the 1930s, specific materials relating to social processes and life functions were too often unavailable and were frequently considered somewhat controversial in their nature. Although there was then a rather general consensus toward what was of value, what was ethical, and so on, social processes and life's functions curricula still tended to raise questions which made many people uncomfortable. Consequently, these curricula were rarely implemented fully but generally reflected the idealistic nature of the individual community.

In many respects the curriculum based on social processes and life functions is the simplest to describe. The movement is associated with the social evolutionist.[9] Therefore, in theory, the curriculum would reflect the values and needs of the existing social order. The task of the schools would be to prepare students with the attitudes and skills necessary to participate in society. In some respects, current emphasis on tasks and job analysis springs from a rationale originally developed in order to justify curricula based on social processes. The purposes and, consequently, the products of task and job analyses differ considerably.

---

[8] O. I. Frederick and L. Farquear, "Areas of Human Activity," *Journal of Educational Research* 30:672-79 (May 1937).

[9] B. Othanel Smith, William O. Stanley, and J. Harlan Shores, *Fundamentals of Curriculum Development* (New York: Harcourt, Brace, 1957), pp. 311-24.

BROAD FIELDS CURRICULUM

Curriculum workers have traditionally accused subject matter specialists of erecting walls between their disciplines as well as between disciplines and the needs of society. The broad fields curriculum attempts to break down the barriers in order to permit an integration of subject matter in a way which relates content masses rather than separates them. The result is the creation of a social studies curriculum that draws upon the disciplines of history, geology, and civics; language arts that includes reading, spelling, composition, and penmanship. Specialized science areas are replaced by broader, survey courses. For example, general biology takes the place of botany and zoology, and general science draws upon the subject areas of the life sciences and the physical sciences. In this way the broad fields curriculum supposedly ignores the lines between disciplines and unifies knowledge in a more functional manner.

In practice the broad fields curriculum is built around unifying laws, principles, and themes that draw from several content areas. The laws and principles approach is most appropriate for the hard sciences; the thematic approach is most prevalent in such fields as language arts and social sciences. In the field of social studies, curricula draw heavily from the work of Harold and Earle Rugg between 1920 and 1928.[10] During this time typical themes were (1) geographic factors influencing economic and social development, (2) the rise of industrialism, (3) technology and cultural development, (4) increasing federal control, and (5) the evolution of democracy.

Many examples of the principles approach to integrating subject areas can be found. In biology, for example, the principle "life has changed, is changing, and will change" can cut across many areas of knowledge. As a matter of fact, the principle has many different aspects, such as cultural and economic, which would probably be included as part of the experience-based curriculum movement. If the principle is related to the study of evolution, which is more typical of the broad fields approach, evidence supporting this principle comes from such fields as genetics, paleontology, geography, comparative anatomy, and embryology.

The aims of an experiment conducted at Benjamin Franklin High School in Los Angeles, California, illustrate what the broad fields curriculum tries to do.

> The instruction aims to pass beyond concern for mere facts and names as such, and strives to determine the bearing of each period of human

[10] Earle Rugg, *Curriculum Studies in the Social Sciences and Citizenship* (Greeley, Colorado: Colorado State Teachers College, 1928).

culture upon our own. To attain this self-understanding the student should build up for himself a picture of the time-sequence of cultures, of their geographical setting, and of their historical developments. This means that into a framework must be set the vivid outlines of the achievements of each age in the organization of society, in literature and art and music, in science and philosophy, in morals and religion. Thus the whole history of human culture is the material from which understanding of civilization and of the human life must come. When the student understands what of good has lived, how worth-while influences make for subsequent conduct and right living, and what forces have been constructive and what destructive, then, and only then, may he make an adequate plan of life for himself.[11]

Much of the activity of curriculum workers has centered around problems associated with isolation and integration of traditional content areas. Themes, generalizations, laws, and principles all need masses of information for their support. Staying on these so-called high levels can fail to produce the details needed for a thorough comprehension. Survey courses have traditionally been criticized because they cover too much ground too quickly to be of much value. The danger is that "broad courses will turn into a passive overview of generalizations which offer little opportunity for active inquiry and active learning."[12]

CORE CURRICULUM

The core curriculum is a response to the criticism that educational programs were growing rapidly and developing in a piecemeal fashion containing lots of discrete but unarticulated entities. Concepts of a basic core of studies were popular at the turn of the century much as they are today. Core curriculum attempts to identify courses or experiences that are essential and to subordinate all other subjects. Early attempts at providing a core of courses too frequently pitted one discipline and the personnel who represented it against others and made little effort to blend the disciplines. Later core developments emphasized social values by establishing problems or themes which relate to the social context and by drawing upon the discrete disciplines in order to solve problems or develop themes. In this respect the core curriculum purported to include the better aspects of other curriculum designs. Fixing the structure of the curriculum by identifying broad social issues relates to the social processes and life functions curriculum, whereas, the supporting content

---

[11] Rose E. Stetler, "An Experiment in Informal Education," *California Journal of Secondary Education* 10:516-17 (Nov. 1935).

[12] Hilda Taba, *Curriculum Development: Theory and Practice* (New York: Harcourt, Brace and World, 1962), p. 395.

cuts across discrete subject areas and creates arrangements not too different than those identified by the broad fields curriculum.

The difference in the aims of the subject curriculum and the core curriculum is in degree. The subject curriculum tends to emphasize competencies that are related to sequential preparation. For instance, a student desiring to become a medical doctor is told that biology, physiology, anatomy, chemistry, and physics are needed in order to understand basic principles of how the body functions. The subject-organized curriculum simply states that in order to do one thing, one must first learn about another. In a way, the core curriculum has attempted to operate on many fronts at the same time by emphasizing a technique of problem identification and resolution. The rationale here is direct: if people are trained to solve their own problems, they will become more self-sufficient individuals and as a consequence better contributors to society. The emphasis in the core curriculum as compared to those of other curricula tends to be in degree rather than in direction. The core curriculum tends to emphasize broad problems and problem-solving techniques, whereas the subject-organized curriculum tends to emphasize preparation as a scientist, medical doctor, engineer, and so forth. Neither movement would deny the usefulness of the other's emphasis, but rather would attempt to show how its configuration would account for the efforts of the other.

Smith, Stanley, and Shores summarize the characteristics of the core curriculum movement by identifying four program elements.[13] First, the curriculum consists of common competencies that are essential for all students. Second, the activities designed to develop the understandings and skills are cooperatively planned by teachers and students. Third, the core curriculum purports to capitalize on the "teachable moment" by making provisions for concentrating on special needs as they appear. Fourth, specific competencies are taught as they are needed rather than taught at the convenience of the curriculum, school, or teacher. This fourth characteristic brings into focus a dilemma that all curriculum workers face, that is, is it better to learn the principles first and then gain experience in practice, or is it better to learn the principles after experience in order to vest the activity with meaning and the principle with concrete evidence and experience?

As is the case in many educational innovations, those who developed and supported the concept of core curriculum tend to account for its failure by complaining that, when critically examined, most programs purporting to employ the core curriculum were in practice doing some-

[13] Smith, Stanley, Shores, *Fundamentals of Curriculum Development,* pp. 311-24.

thing else. By the same token, any attempt to find a school that employed one of the curriculum designs in any ideal sense is nearly impossible. Many schools believed they were employing the core curriculum with great accuracy of both design and intent, but outside experts inevitably viewed these experiments as incomplete models. In other words, schools purporting to implement particular curriculum types seem always to be distorting or misinterpreting what the original designers had in mind. Perhaps the greatest single reason that core curricula were never accepted in practice was that the values representative of the main stream of American culture were not clear and consequently core programs were unable to accurately translate social problems into curriculum themes.

### EXPERIENCE-BASED CURRICULUM

In the case of the experience- or activity-based curriculum, educators generally accept the hypothesis that there is a relationship between the quality of educational experience and the learning that takes place. The diffuse nature of the activity-based movement tends to coalesce around the phrase "reconstruction of experience." Unfortunately, like other key ideas in other curricula, the term "reconstrutcion of experience" has never been functionally developed. The meaning of the phrase is generally taken somewhat superficially and interpreted loosely. The activity movement may be summarized as comprehensive and obscure.

The activity-based curriculum, in an extensive humanitarian effort directed toward making real the American dream, began as a scheme for coordinating the psychological and social factors common to educational problems. In order to accomplish this, the activity-based curriculum required a broad educational program that included a concern for the social and the intellectual life of the child. The movement stressed both vocational and health education as each related to the family and the community. The curriculum attempted to assimilate the many classes of children who were entering the schools and who were demanding a more practical kind of education. Finally, new pedagogical techniques were supposedly utilized in an attempt to organize the curriculum in such a way that a new level of democracy and nationalism could emerge.

The most widely accepted misconception of the activity-based curriculum related to the belief that children's interests dictated the curriculum. This interpretation of the movement is just as fallacious as the concept that freedom allows anyone to do anything he wants. Today, educators accept the fact that sound programs demand that the curriculum be built on the experiential background of the learner. This is also the intent of the activity-based curriculum. "It is further held that children who are intensely and richly engaged in a process of meeting their felt needs are at the same time receiving the best preparation for dealing with the demands later events will make upon them."[14] In other words, the movement purports to capitalize upon the interests, abilities, and experiences of the learner.

Typically, the content of the curriculum centered around interests relating to such categories as (1) home life, (2) the natural world, (3) the community, (4) food production and distribution, (5) transportation and communications, (6) community life of earlier times, (7) community life of other lands and people, and (8) social experience.[15] The assumption that people learn best what they experience associated the activity-based curriculum with problem-solving methods. Since children were encouraged to help set their own tasks and to learn content and skills as they were needed, the curriculum soon became very broadly interpreted by the schools. The central thrust of providing experience that would enable students to reconstruct society, to move further toward the American ideal, frequently became lost by those who saw the movement as endorsing any activity that a student might want to do.

### HUMANISTIC CURRICULUM

Alternative schools as well as counter-culture schools are dramatic attempts to deinstitutionalize the educational process. Although there is a great variation in the purpose and philosophy of many of these new schools, generally speaking, they all share a concern for a more humanistic kind of education. The schools purporting to have a more humanistic curriculum have been called community schools, nonschools, free schools, open schools, storefront schools, and experimental schools. Alternative schools such as the British Infant School tend to operate more within the traditional institution than do counter-culture schools. Consequently, counter-culture schools offer a more genuine alternative to traditional school systems. All schools purporting to be humanistic in nature justify their curricula as being more democratic. That is, members of a democratic society have the right to choose among educational opportunities. The society, therefore, must develop viable alternatives to traditional patterns.

[14] Ibid., p. 293.
[15] Ruth Manning Hockett, *Teachers' Guide to Child Development: Manual for Kindergarten and Primary Teachers* (Sacramento: California State Department of Education, 1930), p. 60.

As is the case in all previous curricula, identifying what each movement is responding to is easier than determining how effective each response has been. Few argue against the necessity of integrating knowledge, of making schools more responsive to human and societal needs, and of humanizing whenever possible.

More specifically, in 1969 the students in Montgomery County, Maryland, produced a document which outlined the dehumanizing effects of the educational institution. The Student Alliance Report identified ten dehumanizing effects perpetuated by the county public schools:

1. Schools are based upon fear which includes receiving bad grades, punishment, humiliation, and ostracism
2. Schools encourage dishonesty since it is necessary for success
3. Students must subvert their desire to respond honestly to questions and develop the skill of feeding the teacher the answer he wants
4. Schools destroy the natural eagerness to learn and discover
5. Schools help students develop feelings of resentment and alienation
6. Schools place a premium on conformity
7. The system stifles self-expression
8. The curriculum is too narrow
9. Because of the lack of free exchange of ideas and life styles, the school system develops prejudice
10. Because school systems label successes and failures they develop self-hate which is cruelly damaging to the student's ego.[16]

A theme which seems to run through concerns such as these has to do with the needs of children and the authority the culture places with adults. The adult should serve as the assistant, the helper, and the model. However, as the child seeks to grow and know himself, the adult often sets arbitrary rules that block development desired by both adults and children. Ideally, the humanitarian movement in education is pleading for the natural and against the artificial and arbitrary elements in the school system.

### PERFORMANCE-BASED CURRICULUM

The best defined and tested curricula are performance-based. This statement can be made for a number of reasons. Some of the first performance-based programs of study were developed by industry and

---

[16] Ronald Gross and Paul Osterman, eds., *High School* (New York: Simon and Schuster, 1971), pp. 108-15.

the military, both of which insisted upon knowing whether or not the instructional sequence produced the performance specified. In other words, technological responsibility was considered as a primary goal of the movement itself. Consequently, a strong research component is built in early to establish the effectiveness of the instructional system employed. Performance goals are designed in rigorous detail before alternative instructional learning activities are evaluated. Learning activities are constantly altered during developmental testing of a performance-based curriculum until the required number of subjects complete the sequence at a specified level of performance. This requires an identification and application of principles of best educational practice. The important implication here is that an instructional sequence is at fault if a specified number of learners are unable to demonstrate competency. This is preferable to putting the blame solely on the learner.

The competencies (knowledge, skills, behaviors) identified in competency-based curricula are role derived. This means that if one is preparing an educational program for students to learn a specific skill then an exemplar in that skill must be observed. This is basic to an understanding of competency-based designs. The content of an experience in writing history, for example, would be derived from a study of the competencies of historians. This concept encourages experiences which allow students to participate in activities typical of a poet, musician, scientist, historian, social worker, business executive, and so on. To use an old cliché, the emphasis is not entirely on what the student knows upon graduation but rather the emphasis is on what a student can do with what he knows.

The most frequently encountered misconception of how competencies are derived in a performance-based educational program relates to the belief that the teacher simply transforms a particular content area into behaviorally designed statements that guide both the learning activities and the evaluation of performance. This literal translation of performance-based concepts misses one of the basic assumptions. The curriculum is determined by desired performance, not by the instructional designer. The instructional designer becomes an analyst of performance and a translator of what he observes.

Elam summarizes the essential characteristics of a performance-based teacher education program:

1. Competencies (knowledge, skills, behaviors) to be demonstrated by the students are derived from explicit conceptions of teacher roles, stated so as to make possible assessment of a student's behavior in relation to specific competencies, and made public in advance.

2. Criteria to be employed in assessing competencies are based upon, and in harmony with, specified competencies; explicit in stating expected levels of mastery under specified conditions; and made public in advance.
3. Assessment of the student's competency uses his performance as the primary source of evidence; takes into account evidence of the student's knowledge relevant to planning for, analyzing, interpreting, or evaluating situations or behaviors; and strives for objectivity.
4. The student's rate of progress through the program is determined by demonstrated competency rather than by time or course completion.
5. The instructional program is intended to facilitate the development and evaluation of the student's achievement of competencies specified.[17]

Performance-based educational programs like the teacher education program described by Stanley Elam apply principles of technological responsibility and best educational practice. Performance-based programs employ scientific processes closely associated with systems approaches. A rational system is technologically responsible because the execution of each step will produce data that can be used to refine the system (empirically derived). The system itself represents one mode of inquiry and is by design a technologically responsible system.

The translation of such a design into an operational system requires the application of principles of best educational practice. Although some still believe that the ideal, technologically responsible system can be teacher proof, institution proof, and entirely directed by the learner, most now agree that such a system is neither feasible nor desirable in a comprehensive sense. The application of a performance-based system requires people who understand and believe in the process and can skillfully make the many arrangements (orchestrate environments) necessary for the development of competencies. For example, most performance-based systems for education professionals must utilize a variety of field centers as educational sites. Anyone managing a program where students must work with a number of professionals and other on-the-job students knows the importance of the art of working with people.

In summary, technological responsibility relates directly to planning as well as to scientific ways and means for collecting and processing data for the purpose of system verification and improvement. As stated in chapter 1, best educational practice is the art of "pulling it off," of vesting the program with personal meaning for each student, of reconciling—on the spot—the many unpredictable occurrences that are inevitable in

---

[17] Stanley Elam, *Performance-Based Teacher Education* (Washington, D.C.: American Association of Colleges for Teacher Education, 1972), pp. 6-7.

order for students to move forward toward the achievement of both personal and program objectives.

The staggering problem of providing an adequate information base for schools as they move from one curriculum design to another has too frequently blocked effective integration and encouraged library media programs to develop independent, bureaucratic structures of their own. Consequently, the media program is usually viewed as a competing entity among other discrete entities in the total educational program, rather than as a necessary component that must function in specific ways if programs are to be developed and implemented. This is particularly evident as academic departments, system-wide divisions, and others involved strive for their slice of the monetary pie.

Certain observations must be made about curricula and media. First, providing media services for curricula such as the broad fields curriculum, the experience-based curriculum, and the core curriculum demands an enormous information base. Each movement tends to define itself so broadly that it becomes synonymous with general education. This not only destroys the usefulness and specific strength of each design, but also mandates reference and recreational collections as well as technological devices that are well out of the reach of many schools. As media professionals live through one curriculum movement after another, each appearing to demand more and more resources, the response tends to be to ask for bigger and bigger media budgets. This condition not only contributes to inevitable dissidence among entities competing for monies, but also seems to drain personnel of energies that should be spent on identifying, refining, and translating each new design into a total, integrated system. This has been too much to expect from personnel who were not trained to look at a total system in relation to its ability to produce identified outcomes.

Second, each curriculum design demands more and more specialization in order for the theory to be translated into practice. Standard preparation programs for media personnel as well as for teachers have insisted upon producing a "basic professional," leaving specialized training for a later date. Since each curriculum movement demands, by design, the incredible job of retraining teachers and supporting staff and administrators as well as reeducating the community, each movement seems doomed before it begins. Sarason discusses the problems of simply reducing class size, which is only one seemingly minor problem that schools must face in order to implement some of the proposed curriculum designs.

One of the most frequent fantasies in which teachers indulge—and it is by no means restricted to teachers—is how enjoyable life in a classroom could be if class size were discernibly decreased. . . . if Congress in its infinite wisdom were to pass legislation making it financially possible to cut class size in half, the legislation could not be implemented. It is conceivable that over a period of a decade the necessary physical plant could be built—our society has rarely failed in crash programs of a technological nature. What would be impossible would be to train teachers and other educational specialists in the numbers necessary to implement the legislation. . . . the goal of dramatically reducing class size is far from a financial problem.[18]

The problems of each curriculum movement as related to personnel, material, and facility needs are infinitely more complex than simply reducing class size. The problem of redirecting institutions for preparing personnel to implement a new curriculum is staggering. At the end of each era, the few institutions that have managed to develop programs for the preparation of professionals for a curriculum then in vogue find themselves obsolete once more.

The implication for media specialists and media programs seems obvious. Media programs are designed to provide better ways and means for a wide range of curriculum strategies that fit many philosophical frames while at the same time meeting the specific requirements of the school curriculum at any point in time.

Third, in order for any enterprise to be developed to the point that it can be realistically tested, it must have clear-cut, commonly understood purposes. Although each curriculum movement has its founding fathers, in every case the purposes have been viewed differently, changed significantly, and applied as they could be when the plans were put into action. Educating is like playing a game. In order to win, one must know the object of the game. The culture has repeatedly emphasized what they expect of their schools. Broadly speaking, concerns center around concepts of acculturation and self-actualization. The trick is to develop schools that are manned by professionals who contribute something unique and yet know how their particular effort increases the ability of individuals to benefit from and contribute to society in such a way that they feel they are consistently extending their best efforts. Each curriculum movement has contributed to the effort in one way or another but has failed in its attempt to be *the* answer.

Fourth, the organization of the curriculum theoretically must accommodate the functions necessary for the educational enterprise to realize

---

[18] Seymour B. Sarason, *The Creation of Settings and the Future Societies* (San Francisco: Jossey-Bass, 1972), p. 99.

its purposes. This has seemingly been impossible. Each design has had to be implemented using the personnel, materials, and facilities that existed in any paricular school. The continuance of the textbook as well as the classroom testify to the fact that curriculum movements of the past have not progressed far enough to change firm, basic patterns. Schools have traditionally accepted theoretically new designs under the assumption that a little in-service and a few more materials are all that are needed to change direction.

In summary, the abundant literature which relates to curriculum can be interpreted to show how the failure of each movement is the result of its general nature and consequently its inability to identify, develop, and utilize principles of best educational practice and technological responsibility in any unique sense. This is to say that each movement can be described in general terms more easily than in terms of the tools and techniques that were developed and verified. Hence, a study of curriculum movements is largly descriptive by nature. Each movement represented a response to the context (society). If the psychological, sociological, and philosophical tenor of each era is adequately represented in the literature, then it is reasonable that each curriculum movement has been an honest and intelligent response to the context. In simpler terms, the rationale expounded by each of the founding fathers caught the imaginations of those concerned with the schools and thus gained the support necessary for reform. Nevertheless, each curriculum movement has had its impact on the thinking of professionals as well as on programs that currently exist in the schools. The problem is in determining what the impact has been.

Breaking down subject matter lines and attempting to realistically integrate knowledge with the needs of students have been identified frequently as positive residual effects of the various curriculum movements. Others point to the frustration and alienation that each new movement brings. Undoubtedly the positive and negative impact of each new movement has *modified* the schools. Saying much more than this, however, is very difficult since the literature tends to reflect individual attitudes, perceptions, testimony, and judgments rather than controlled, objective analyses of the impact of each design.

## Implications for the Media Program

1. Teachers and administrators oriented toward a particular curriculum movement will express an attitude toward the general thrust of an educational program. When media personnel disagree, the ensuing philosophical dialogue may be self-defeating. A better posture is to en-

courage the use of specific modes of inquiry that transcend the concerns of broad curriculum movements.

2. Media personnel should make every attempt to help diversify the modes of inquiry utilized in curriculum implementation.

3. Regardless of the number of subjects offered in a particular educational program, or the way they are grouped, or the way subject material is utilized, media professionals must understand the reasons and be able to build media programs that relate to the educational program of which they are a part.

4. Some modes of inquiry relate better to one discipline than to another. In addition, some teachers and students will prefer one mode over another. For example, reviewing the periodical literature as part of a formal research paper requires reference as well as abstracting and writing skills. This mode is more likely to be employed by the history or science teacher than the art teacher. On the other hand, the art teacher may send a student to the media center to study a period in art history or to explore specific techniques, such as those employed by wood block printers, for the purpose of applying some of these techniques in the art class. The media specialist should support, assist, and suggest various ways of approaching problems unique to the modes of inquiry students and teachers are employing.

5. Curricula emphasizing social processes and general themes require media collections that take into account the general goals as well as provide a variety of materials in appropriate numbers for each topic. Modes of inquiry used to develop each topic have implications for collections development, media center utilization, and media program integration with a particular aspect of the curriculum.

6. Media professionals must encourage students and teachers to discuss specific problems, assignments, and materials if they are to understand how the media program can assist, extend, and initiate activities that coincide with the curriculum. Such dialogues can bring the media program closer to the curriculum and can provide information for further development. Dialogue must be coupled with careful observation, with a comparison of what is being done with what is said to be going on.

7. The application of best educational practice and technological responsibility relates to the level of sophistication of the educational delivery system as well as to the appropriate matching of modes of inquiry to teacher-learning tasks. The specific techniques that students, teachers, and media professionals learn to employ will carry over from one curriculum movement to the next succeeding one.

**Problems and Activities for Research and Discussion**

1. After reading the references indicated, formulate and defend your individual definition of the school curriculum.

Anderson, Vernon E. *Principles and Procedures of Curriculum Improvement.* 2nd ed. New York: Ronald Pr., 1965, pp. 1–85.

Foshay, Arthur W. *Curriculum for the 70's: An Agenda for Invention.* Washington, D.C.: National Education Association, Center for Study of Instruction, 1970, pp. 28–32.

Kelley, Earl C. *Education for What is Real.* New York: Harper, 1947, pp. 82–90.

Saylor, K. Galen, and Alexander, William M. *Curriculum Planning.* New York: Holt, Rinehart and Winston, 1966, pp. 3–43.

Taba, Hilda. *Curriculum Development: Theory and Practice.* New York: Harcourt, Brace and World, 1962, pp. 9–10.

Trump, J. Lloyd, and Miller, Delmas F. *Secondary School Curriculum Improvement.* Boston: Allyn and Bacon, 1968, pp. 3–40.

2. After reading the references indicated, prepare a model illustrating the interrelated steps of the curriculum planning process.

Boles, Harold W. *Step by Step to Better School Facilities.* New York: Holt, Rinehart and Winston, 1965, pp. 3–83.

Cyrs, Thomas E., Jr., and Lowenthal, Rita. "A Model for Curriculum Design Using a Systems Approach," *Audiovisual Instruction* 15: 16–18 (Jan. 1970).

Taba, Hilda. *Curriculum Development: Theory and Practice.* New York: Harcourt, Brace and World, 1962, pp. 438–44.

3. List three possible strategies that could assist in the solution of each of the seven problems identified under "Problems of General Curriculum Theory and Development."

4. Cite three factors that blocked successful implementation of each of the general curriculum movements discussed.

5. Discuss the term *component dissonance* as related to three levels of curriculum development—school and district, university, and commercial.

6. Generate a list of ten ways the media specialist can become involved with curriculum work. (Example: Attend department meetings.)

7. A teacher friend tells the media specialist that a university supervisor of student teachers "makes her so mad she can hardly see straight." It seems that the supervisor asked the teacher what she taught and she replied, "Sophomore English." The supervisor said that he hoped she taught "sophomore students." Can these two points of view be mediated? Does each reflect an attitude toward the curriculum?

Curricular and Technological Innovations

PROBLEM. The media program must not only accommodate current curriculum designs but also provide ways and means of solving problems unique to a particular school and district. Media professionals must constantly be looking for more appropriate tools and techniques that will allow them to contribute positively to the problem solving process. Those who keep themselves in the vanguard of educational change constantly evaluate innovations in terms of implications for media programs. A working knowledge of curricular and technological innovations is an asset to media professionals as they seek viable alternatives for their programs.

The purpose of this module is to acquaint media professionals with a number of curricular and technological innovations that have potential for educational and media program improvement. The list is by no means exhaustive, but rather illustrative of the many innovations currently a part of the educational scene.

OBJECTIVES. Given the following list of innovations,

(1) locate two sources of information,

(2) formulate a description, and

(3) suggest an implication for the media program for each innovation listed.

> British Infant School
> Cable television
> Continuous progress
> Criterion referenced test
> Data processing
> DATRIX
> Delphi
> Digital communication networks
> EPIE
> ERIC
> IGE
> Interaction analysis
> IPI
> Laser beams
> Learning contract

MARC tapes
MEDLINE
NCLIS
NICEM
PLAN
PLATO
PROMOD
QUERY
Storefront schools
Ultrafiche

## REFERENCES

Aiken, Henry D. *The Age of Ideology.* New York: Macmillan, 1932.

Anderson, Vernon E. *Principles and Procedures of Curriculum Improvement.* 2nd ed. New York: Ronald Pr., 1965.

Bayles, Ernest E. *Democratic Educational Theory.* New York: Harper, 1960.

Boles, Harold W. *Step by Step to Better School Facilities.* New York: Holt, Rinehart and Winston, 1965.

Breed, Frederick S. *Education and the New Realism.* New York: Macmillan, 1939.

Broudy, Harry S. *The Real World of the Public Schools.* New York: Harcourt Brace Jovanovich, 1972.

Broudy, Harry S., Smith, B. Othanel, and Burnett, Joe R. *Democracy and Excellence in Secondary Education.* Chicago: Rand McNally, 1964.

Brubacher, John S., ed. *Modern Philosophies and Education.* Chicago: National Society for the Study of Education, 1955.

Cordasco, Francesco. *A Brief History of Education.* Paterson, N.J.: Littlefield, Adams, 1963.

Cyrs, Thomas E., Jr., and Lowenthal, Rita. "A Model for Curriculum Design Using a Systems Approach." *Audiovisual Instruction* 15:16-18 (Jan. 1970).

Elam, Stanley. *Performance-Based Teacher Education.* Washington, D.C.: American Association of Colleges for Teacher Education, 1972.

Foshay, Arthur W. *Curriculum for the 70's: An Agenda for Invention.* Washington, D.C.: National Education Association, Center for Study of Instruction, 1970.

Frederick, O. I., and Farquear, L. "Areas of Human Activity." *Journal of Educational Research* 30:672-79 (May 1937).

Gross, Ronald, ed. *The Teacher and the Taught: Education in Theory and Practice from Plato to James B. Conant.* New York: Dell, 1963.

Gross, Ronald, and Osterman, Paul, eds. *High School.* New York: Simon and Schuster, 1971.

Hertzberg, Hazel W. *Historical Parallels for the Sixties and Seventies: Primary Sources and Core Curriculum Revisited.* ERIC Microfiche, ED 51-066.

Hockett, Ruth Manning. *Teachers' Guide to Child Development: Manual for Kindergarten and Primary Teachers.* Sacramento: California State Department of Education, 1930.

Holt, John. *What Do I Do Monday?* New York: Dutton, 1970.

Kelley, Earl C. *Education for What Is Real.* New York: Harper, 1947.

Oettinger, Anthony G., and Zapol, Nikki. "Will Information Technologies Help Learning?" *Teachers College Record* 74:5-54 (Sept. 1972).

Phenix, Philip H. "The Architectonics of Knowledge." In *Education and the Structure of Knowledge.* Ed. Stanley Elam. Chicago: Rand McNally, 1964, pp. 44-74.

Redden, J. D., and Ryan, F. A. *A Catholic Philosophy of Education.* Milwaukee: Bruce, 1942.

Rugg, Earle. *Curriculum Studies in the Social Sciences and Citizenship.* Greeley: Colorado State Teachers College, 1928.

Sarason, Seymour B. *The Creation of Settings and the Future Societies.* San Francisco: Jossey-Bass, 1972.

Saylor, J. Galen, and Alexander, William M. *Curriculum Planning.* New York: Holt, Rinehart and Winston, 1966.

Smith, B. Othanel, Stanley, William O., and Shores, J. Harlan. *Fundamentals of Curriculum Development.* New York: Harcourt, Brace, 1957.

Stetler, Rose E. "An Experiment in Informal Education." *California Journal of Secondary Education* 10:516-17 (Nov. 1935).

Taba, Hilda. *Curriculum Development: Theory and Practice.* New York: Harcourt, Brace and World, 1962.

Trump, J. Lloyd, and Miller, Delmas F. *Secondary School Curriculum Improvement.* Boston: Allyn and Bacon, 1968.

Ulich, Robert. *The Human Career.* New York: Harper, 1955.

# Toward a Total Design

THE HISTORY of man may be viewed as a continuous struggle to bring the environment under control, to establish order and purpose. Man, like his institutions, develops power by establishing some relationships and discouraging others, by trading freedom in one order for liberty in another, by establishing a symbiotic relationship with biological, mechanical, psychological, sociological, and philosophical environments. The freedom trade-off exists everywhere—the farmer and hybrid wheat, the pilot and his plane, man and his perception of self, the judge and justice, and man and his religion. The power-vulnerability of a person or institution is ascertained by determining how other elements in the environment are influenced by the person or institution and vice versa.

Whatever form the evaluation of school media programs in relation to total programs may take, sooner or later the adequacy of school media programs in the context of schools and society has to be considered in terms of their relative effectiveness and efficiency (trade-off). With this end in mind, general systems theory, a science of wholeness, provides a view of the school media program as it functions in the educational program and in society. As a result, the security of an educational program must be expressed in the degree to which society is dependent on the educational system. The better society can see the specific functions schools perform, the more credible the educational program; the more obscure the functions, the more fragile the relationship between schools and society. In turn, the media program is a systematic group of experiences providing ways and means for students to achieve educational

45

outcomes. If purposes and informational links between the educational program and the media program are blurred, security may take the form of a closed, independent system which functions for self-preservation rather than as an extension of the society of which it is a part. The purpose of a system provides meaning for its existence, whereas information provides the raw material for translating desires into action and establishing control.

### THE SYSTEMS CONTEXT

In general systems theory, every system must exist for a purpose. Though systems approaches are sometimes considered cold, mechanistic, mathematical models, they are more appropriately processes that enable man to achieve his purposes. Systems approaches have penetrated into almost all aspects of the human endeavor. Unfortunately, the popularity currently enjoyed by systems theory has tended to overshadow some of the central principles. One basic problem is the overpromoted idea that almost anything is a system, an idea which seems to invite people to define a system in any way they like.

General systems theory is an attempt to define wholeness by studying the entity as it exists as a functioning totality. The concept of the whole child is, in a sense, a systems theory. Those who find meaning in general systems theory, as well as those who feel education must relate to the whole child, are struggling to find reasons for performing varous specific functions. The common sense argument that a person will do a task if he understands why the task is important seems to be an application of this basic belief. General systems theory underscores the necessity for developing purposes, for translating purposes and operational objectives into necessary functions, for identifying components necessary to perform each function, and for establishing information feedback systems for monitoring and controlling the system.

In a similar way, organismic biology is an attempt to view living forms as functioning entities. General systems theory, whole child pedagogy, and organismic biology, therefore, are all operating under similar assumptions and constraints. Each field is criticized by those who argue that the sum of the parts does not make up the whole. This typical criticism reflects a common misunderstanding of general systems theory. Although identifying and understanding the parts that make up the whole are important, the interrelationships between the parts hold the key to the understanding of wholeness.

Because systems techniques have been applied most frequently to isolated functions such as budgeting, acquisitioning, and retrieving information, the frequent observation is that systems tend to neglect the more important humanistic aspects of media or educational programs. Industrial corporations engaged in performance contracting tend to give credence to this assumption, for performance contractors have developed systems of instruction in response to demands. School districts, however, have not been hiring performance contractors to develop the affective dimensions of their programs. Unfortunately, there seems to be evidence to indicate that although educational planners like to talk about their interests in developing educational programs to meet the needs of the whole child, when it is time to budget the money, reading takes preference over the fine arts program, mathematics takes precedence over developing activities designed to provide practice in social skills, and grammar is apt to enjoy more support than creative writing or drama. As long as humanistic aspects of acculturation and self-actualization are low on the list of priorities, technology for promoting them and methods for applying the technology will not be developed. Nevertheless, it is reasonable to assume that a systems outlook can be as useful in developing education for affective growth as for cognitive development.

The development of languages and symbols testifies to the fact that from the very beginning humans and their technologies have been partners. People have progressed because they have been able to build upon what others have done. Cultures have been able to extend their capabilities through the invention and utilization of tools and techniques. Although it is debatable whether or not some prehistoric person intelligently chose the first tool or simply stumbled on the implement by accident, there is little doubt about modern culture's careful and deliberate search for technological devices. As people attempt to understand and control themselves and their environments, they gradually move from an era utilizing trial and error as a method for technological inventing to an era emphasizing technique for creating devices to further augment a human's basic capabilities. In this era, with a specialized adaption of the scientific method called general systems theory, media specialists are beginning to take a fresh look at their functions as they relate to the total educational endeavor.

The evolution of systems may be analyzed as a series of changing subsystems organized to support a dynamic culture (suprasystem). As a system evolves, the technology becomes wedded to the culture and contributes to the irreversibility of change. The evolution of a system incorporates a series of events occurring in a particular setting and triggering change. Understanding change entails the identification of the incidents that cause change. In this regard, there seems to be an interesting similarity between biological evolution and sociological evolution. During biological evolution certain events—such as change in the environment (setting)—trigger adaptation mechanisms in the organism. When the organism has evolved to the next stage, it cannot return to its original patterns. (Theoretically, the species could revert to an earlier pattern, although the mathematical probability is not worth considering.) So it seems to be with social systems, especially in reference to institutions; it is impossible to recapture the past in order to respond to the present or to anticipate the future.

In a sense, all change can be defined as a process whereby new entities and new combinations of existing entities are formed. This concept may account for some of the difficulty encountered as school systems attempt to meet the increasing demands placed on them by society and as school media programs attempt to respond to the needs of modern educational programs. The combination of specialities, materials, facilities, and processes needed to implement programs that meet the developmental needs of the whole child just may not exist in schools as we know them. If this is the case, shifting the basic elements could never produce the desired results. Schools may be in the same bind as the old alchemist when he tried to turn lead into gold: what he needed was a cyclotron, not a mortar and pestle.

In spite of the lack of functional organization, any phenomenon or enterprise may be studied as a system. First, an objective analysis of interrelating parts is carefully constructed. Entities or components within the system are rarely able to see the whole. As a consequence, those groups or programs attempting to examine the systems of which they are a part are rarely able to accurately account for existing functional relationships. Besides, the person who studies the system of which he is a part is apt to give preference to his purposes over the purpose for the existence of the system. Systems that have weak informational links with their context tend to evolve in such a way that they reflect the ambitions and purposes of the people in control. This point is simple but all-important because the school media program can function in such a way to perpetuate itself at the expense of the learner's needs.

There is an important difference between the evolution of a system politically and functionally. Political evolution tends to involve changes representing compromises to appease people in power and to increase power. By keeping purposes, means, and ends blurred, political changes are facilitated. One example of political change is redesignating the organization and changing the descriptions of an educational program to make it appear up-to-date but leaving the functions the same. Functional evolution, on the other hand, tends to be more empirically based. Functional changes are made among alternatives in order to increase the system's probability and efficiency in achieving clearly defined purposes. For example, restructuring the role of the media specialist and teacher may follow recognition of the need for certain modes of inquiry.

### A SYSTEMS VIEW OF THE SCHOOL MEDIA PROGRAM

School media programs do not simply sprout up like mushrooms, but rather represent an expenditure of funds for people and physical components assembled for the purpose of providing constructive alternatives for curricular activities. Even though school media programs come into existence because of intelligent decision making, the means utilized to achieve the identified goals and objectives must be constantly examined. Media specialists are becoming increasingly sensitive to the vast amount of know-how that exists to help in determining both means and ends. Of particular significance to the planning of media services is the systems approach. Man has always developed systems for interacting with his environment, and today he is using a system for the study of the system he has chosen for achieving his end.

As stated before, the relationships and the order among the entities are what accurately account for a system. In other words, a school media program may be defined as a logical configuration of the significant elements that not only accurately account for the whole but also describe the relationships among components, systems, and their suprasystem. The term *logical* is used to account for the interrelationships that exist among entities which enable the establishment of a system for the communication among and between entities as well as with its suprasystem. In the case of a school media program, logical must also be used to describe a process of formal reasoning as well as the anticipated intuition a media specialist gains through experience. The educational system differs from natural systems such as the solar system in that the educational system must function in an integrated manner in order to attain manmade, predetermined objectives. The same is the case for the school media program, which is a synthetic assemblage and can be recognized only after its specific purposes are made known.

The purposes and objectives of the school media program, like the total educational program, are dependent upon the support of personnel, materials, equipment, facilities, processes, and content. The whole system must function in harmony for a mutual purpose. The roles people play reflect their knowledge, skills, and attitudes as they contribute to the realization of program objectives. Students, teachers, media specialists, administrative personnel, and community persons are examples of entities that account for the necessary human component of any program.

The school media program must have clearly stated operational objectives and be limited by them. Objectives must be frequently reviewed in order to prevent the erosion and distortion that may occur over time. Individuals tend to forget objectives once they have been established and also to interpret objectives to serve individual purposes. Contemporary school media programs must increasingly bring users into direct contact with the objectives of the programs they enter as well as familiarize them with documents, films, and other learning materials in order for them to predict, control, and regulate information needed and received.

Carefully planned and utilized feedback should be used for auditing the school media program. The special variety of feedback in schools and in school media programs is called evaluation. The measurement of a school media program's effectiveness will include:

1. expert opinion—how complete and appropriate is the media program?
2. achievement indicators—how well does the media program meet curriculum specifications and individual user wants and needs?
3. student and staff attitudes—how do the students, staff, administration, and community persons feel about the learning experiences provided by the media program?
4. direct observation—what are the appropriate roles of a differentiated staff, of the participating students, of the administrative staff, and of the community as each relates to the school media program?

There are at least four characteristics of a systems approach to a school media program. First, the program is viewed as a whole. Second, the organizational structure follows identified functions within the program. Third, all manpower, materials, and facilities are selected to fit the tasks, not the tasks to them. Fourth, the program changes as the educational program of which it is a part changes.

VIEWING THE SCHOOL MEDIA PROGRAM AS A WHOLE

Wholeness can be achieved only to the extent that purposefulness can be achieved. That is, the more specific the operational parameters of the educational media program, the more directiveness and order. Conversely, the more obscure the purpose, the more random functions appear. Both efficiency and commitment are highly related to the degree purposes are identified. The establishment of commitment pushes very close to a kind of mysterious, supernatural, religious endeavor. Regardless of the teleological implications of purposeful behavior, it is impossible to discover wholeness unless this matter of commitment is considered. Indeed, commitment occurs because individual purposes are congruent with system purposes.

As the school media program attempts to penetrate all aspects of the educational program, visibility is diffused. Consequently, when the media center is "that room down the hall," it is easy to see what it is and what it is not. However, when the media program penetrates all aspects of the educational program, it assumes functions and responsibilities formerly associated with the activities of teachers. This integration can be dangerous in an age screaming for accountability if the media program appears to disappear due to its diffusion in the curriculum.

*Job descriptions.* In order to establish the dependent relationships generated as the media program fuses with the ongoing activities of the curriculum, carefully written rationales, task or job descriptions, and accountability systems must be devised. For example, job descriptions clarify and make visible the roles people play. These descriptions include duties arranged in logical order from observations, interviews, questionnaires, record inspections and logs, and a combination of these data-capturing techniques. When a job description is set down, both the uniqueness and interrelatedness of an individual role become clearer.

*Accountability.* Audits of the media management and administration function, including job descriptions and information collected from users, contribute to the accountability of the media program for any given school. Audits are cooperatively conducted with both district and school level personnel. Five broad areas are covered in these audits. First, the immediate objectives and long-range plans of the media program are evaluated. Second, the policies and procedures of the program are studied. Third, the organizational structure is ascertained. Fourth, personnel are viewed in terms of their functions as well as their needs, the latter including space, equipment, and materials enabling efficient performance of identified functions. Fifth, a careful analysis is made of the methods that management and administration use for control. Facilitative management and administration—approaches that nurture rather than coerce—are critical to the growth, development, and control of functions and operations. In order to audit management and administration functions, information is collected to determine the impact of the media program on the total educational program. From the information collected, a description of the whole program is synthesized.

Although national, state, and local organizations may have check lists and evaluative instruments, assessment of a particular program is probably best accomplished by translating, synthesizing, and preparing procedures for data capture that relate specifically to the program in question. The following questions are typical of those asked about program objectives, and short- and long-range planning as they relate to management and administration:

1. Is there a written statement of program objectives and short- and long-range plans as each relates to the media program?
2. Is there a written statement of how program objectives and short- and long-range plans support, enrich, and/or replace parts of the educational program?
3. What procedures were utilized in formulating objectives and plans?
4. Are there adequate procedures for refining and changing both objectives and plans?

Media programs without carefully written policies and procedures rarely function as effectively as they could. The following are examples of appropriate questions frequently asked about the policies and procedures of media programs:

1. Are the policies and procedures available to users in written form?
2. How are exceptions to the policies and procedures made?
3. Do the policies and procedures facilitate the implementation of program objectives?
4. What is the process for establishing policies and procedures utilized in the media program?
5. How are policies and procedures enforced?

The organization of a school and district media program accounts for functions and operations of the total program and makes visible the way the program is set up to achieve its objectives. The following questions may be asked of media program organization:

1. Is there an organizational chart?
2. Does the organizational chart specify who is responsible for what and to whom?
3. Do media program personnel have access to and understand the organizational chart?
4. Are the position titles in the organization suggestive of the generic function of each position?
5. Does the organization encourage free communication on and between all levels?
6. Is the organization flexible, allowing for ad hoc, task-oriented structures?
7. Does the organization rely on cooperative decision making on and between all levels?

To say that a well-developed media program must have adequate numbers of well-trained personnel is axiomatic. To say that the staff of a media program should be motivated, committed, efficient, and innovative is also axiomatic. Although many of these characteristics may be associated with people who are dedicated to the purposes of the school media program, there are other kinds of facilitating conditions that may also be reviewed. The following questions concerning personnel may be asked in order to better formulate a picture of the total program:

1. Can personnel remember, defend, and elaborate on the policies and procedures established by the media program?
2. Does the staff of the media program possess the variety of expertise needed to implement program objectives?
3. Is the general layout of the media center adequate for the efficient functioning of personnel?
4. What is the general condition of the building, the center, its equipment, and materials?
5. Are the materials, machines, and spaces adequate for the identified needs of the users?

The controls that management and administration use in order to insure that program objectives are met must evolve as part of the total plan. Many morale problems exist in schools because management insists on making countless exceptions. Policies, procedures, rules, and regulations should be appropriate for the majority of users and functions. In principle, there must be an exception to every rule. However, if the number of exceptions exceeds the number of times the rule is appropriate, the rule should be changed. The following questions suggest the kinds of considerations that reflect facilitative management and administration:

1. Are procedures for control outlined in the policies and procedures manual?
2. What are the principles utilized to develop means of control?
3. Do management and administration provide adequate lead time for occasional and routine functions?
4. What system do management and administration use to establish standards for control?
5. What procedures do management and administration use to articulate functions and objectives?
6. Do management and administration provide adequate positive reinforcers for sustained high level performance?
7. How do management and administration obtain feedback from all interested populations concerning appropriate aspects of the media program?
8. How do management and administration relate to the district and community?

*Gathering information.* In order to view any organization as a whole, careful plans must be made for information collections. Familiar methods include criterion measure, questionnaires, observation, interviews, inspection of records and logs, and standardized measures. An illustration of each data-capturing technique will show how the technique may be used in an attempt to ascertain what is going on in a particular media program.

To assess specific program objectives *criterion measures* may be used. For example, one objective of the media program might be that every student in school can demonstrate his ability to use the card catalog. The objective should state under what conditions and in what manner the students would be tested for this skill. After this has been determined, the ways and means for checking performance are classed as the criterion measure. For example, students must be able to locate in the card catalog ninety percent of the authors, titles, and subjects requested. The criterion measure will reveal to those interested how close the media program comes to meeting the standard.

When a small amount of information is required from a large number of people, *questionnaires* are valuable. Obviously, questions that provide unnecessary information should be eliminated and the best choice of format must be made. For example, one might ask a user if he finds the material he needs in the media center. If a multiple choice format is used, the student might check "usually," "seldom," or "never" and the media specialist might find that the majority of the students in the school seldom find the materials that they need. Of what value is this information? To ask students to list the materials they needed that they could not find in the media center would be more useful. Be as specific as possible. Because many people object to answering questionnaires, a careful consideration of other methods must be made.

Media professionals need to be keen observers and tactful interviewers if they are going to gain the information they need for smooth-running, efficient media programs. Like all other fact-finding methods, *observations and interviews* should be conducted for a purpose. Most of what a media professional knows about the operation of the media center and its programs is the result of his constant observation of the ongoing activities. A structured observation differs from a casual observation in the degree to which purposes are identified, techniques are determined, and objectivity is sought. One often used observational technique is checking the frequency of a particular category of behavior. Why users come to the media center can be ascertained by observing what they do when they get there. This may be preferable to interviewing, since students may be prone to reflect what they think they should be doing rather than what they are actually doing.

Observational and interviewing techniques vary and are frequently either too broad and simplistic or unduly complicated. Care should be taken, therefore, to build a sound background of theory and knowledge about specific observing and interviewing techniques as data-capturing devices. Both techniques can be carried on constantly and almost unconsciously by media professionals who have developed skills in using these techniques. The following questions illustrate the kinds of problems posed by structured observations:

1. Has the observer made a search of the literature in order to ascertain what is known about what he intends to do?
2. Can the critical variables be isolated for study?
3. What checks for insuring objectivity have been established?
4. Do the behaviors occur frequently enough to make observation practical?[1]

The great advantage of interviewing is that it usually permits in-depth inquiry into a particular situation. There are at least three specific reasons for interviewing. First, the media specialist may discover new facts, opinions, and attitudes. Second, the media professional is able to check and verify information. Third, and possibly most important, interviewing techniques can assist the media professional in meeting and overcoming resistance to the media program. An interview with a dissatisfied faculty member is a situation that media specialists must expect to face many times. The objective of such an interview should never be to win an argument, but rather to establish rapport which has either been lost or never been gained.

Before conducting an interview, the media specialist should review the many techniques and considerations that have been developed for this purpose. Interviewers frequently disclose their own biases through leading questions which tend to prescribe an answer. For example, a question such as "You *do* see the necessity of having a browsing section in the media center?" is much easier to answer in the affirmative. A better question would be, "In what way do your students use the browsing collection of the media center?"

The media professional should never waste the time of others by using questionnaires, observations, or interviews to find out already recorded and available information. Far too many questions are asked of people when a simple *record inspection*—involving a detailed counting of items, entries, documents, services, people—would provide the answer to the interested party. Such an inspection of the records can also yield infor-

[1] Walter R. Borg, *Educational Research: an Introduction* (New York: David McKay, 1963), p. 243.

mation about such things as materials, usage, trends, and personnel work loads.

For comparing and ranking subjects as well as for estimating the potential contributions of new employees or for comparing certain aspects of one media program with others, *standardized measures* are useful. However, comparative studies using standardized measures are more apt to occur on the state or national level than they are in the local school. The need for the media professional to be familiar with the standardized measures utilized in a particular school system is probably dependent upon the degree to which the media professional is involved in a district-wide testing program.

In most cases where a media professional is interested in evaluating staff, program, and/or students, criterion-referenced measures will be more useful than standardized measures. Criterion measures demand that targets be identified, priorities be set, and ways and means for attaining and evaluating progress be provided. For example, in one year the media program may concentrate a portion of its resources on the development and installation of an auto-tutorial experience in materials preparation for students. Developing and installing an operational system are the targets. The ability of students to perform in the way initially described (objectives) becomes the criterion measure. A more simple example would be a program that has as one of its goals (target) a twenty percent increase in film circulation. The criterion is the twenty percent increase; a simple records inspection will reveal whether the criterion has been met.

Information is collected to ascertain the nature of a media program: its description and its impact on a particular situation; its functions; its weaknesses in performance, material, machine, and facility support. Information may also prompt immediate action by correcting or changing procedures during an on-the-spot observation and/or interview. Furthermore, collected information can provide support and suggest directions for short- and long-range planning.

In summary, information contributes to an understanding of wholeness. Wholeness includes a statement of purpose, the ways and means purposes are translated into functions, and the ways and means functions define the components of the educational media program. Short- and long-range planning translates the ideals and aspirations of the staff into a plan for action. The discrepancy between what one wants the school media program to do and what it is doing brings into focus those areas where priorities must be established.

### ORGANIZATIONAL STRUCTURE AFTER IDENTIFIED FUNCTIONS

The way a particular educational system's media program is organized to achieve the system's purposes will vary according to the functions and operations identified. Much of the concern of today's students and critics of education is the way educational systems are organized to achieve their aims. The organization of libraries, educational systems, state agencies, and so on may block their own aims. Many examples can be cited that support the accusation that institutions are organized more efficiently for self-preservation than for service to society. Likewise, many specific examples may be given to show how instructional situations or organizations block objectives. For instance, many believe that the school experience should provide practice in democracy. If this is one of the objectives of an educational program, then the organization of the institution must facilitate the realization of this objective. Yet, if one looks at what is happening rather than at what educators say they are doing, a perplexing situation frequently comes into view. The contradiction can be seen in civics classes which set up artificial situations that preach the tenets of democracy in an authoritarian setting. How can students know and feel the essence of what it means to be a member of a democratic society in a setting that negates the principles advocated?

The hypothesis is that the problems most threatening to schools, school media programs, and even society are organizational. Fortunately, the young people of our nation seem to have lost some of the traditional preoccupation of Americans with material progress and have brought back into focus the necessity for identifying purposes. Youth today are saying that organization fosters feelings of alienation, that organization blocks equal opportunities for all, and that organization obstructs rather than facilitates a new humanistic morality. Students using media centers frequently feel that centers are organized to protect materials rather than to make them available, that centers select what they want students to see and hear rather than what interests them most, and that centers tend to avoid rather than to reach out to those who most need their services.

Technological responsibility must be judged in terms of the ability of technology to free individuals from the authoritarian constraints in education and to further a democratic organizational structure. The central purpose for the existence of any educational system is to facilitate learning and at the same time to improve the quality of life for each individual. If the greater environment, the home-community-society, advances to the point that learning may be made easier to a greater degree and is more humane than the schools themselves, then the educational establishment relinquishes its status as a technologically responsible entity. In other words, educational institutions must provide a more intensive, efficient, humane environment than society at large if they are to justify their existence.

If educators can agree that schools should provide more facilitative environments for learning than a student could reasonably expect to find elsewhere, then the functions and components of an educational system should be directed toward identifying and establishing such an environment. Finding a clear rationale for why men, materials, and processes exist is often difficult. For example, millions and millions of dollars are being spent to collect information about students, and additional millions are spent on providing guidance personnel to utilize this information while working with students. The expense and effort for this must be weighed against the expenditure of resources in other directions. What are the purposes of collecting data and developing guidance programs? What are the alternatives? What do guidance personnel do in traditional programs? What should they do? How does this relate to better educational programs? The abolishment of guidance service is not advocated, but the point is that each function and each component must be carefully analyzed in relation to the purposes of an educational program, with an eye toward spending money in the most efficient and effective manner.

*Functional analysis.* A *functional analysis* determines what is to be done and how it is to be done. A component analysis ascertains who or what can do the job.

The functions of a media program may be considered as management and administration, design, information, and consultation. Each of these functions relates to such operations as acquisition, production, reference, storage and retrieval, evaluation, research and development, maintenance, and distribution. These are examples of what is to be done. Figure 1 represents a systems approach to how each function and operation is done.

For example, the management and administration function has *objectives* that must be *translated* into terms suitable for analysis, taking into consideration the *constraints* under which management and administration must operate. Constraints are distinguished from *variables* that may be manipulated to arrive at *alternatives* that have the potential of achieving objectives. Since both efficiency and effectiveness are considerations in selecting among alternatives, *trade-off* studies are conducted in order to produce data for making choices. The *synthesis* stage organizes the many alternatives selected for each objective identified in the management and administration function. The function has to build in data collecting mechanisms in order to *improve* the alternatives employed for reaching objectives as well as selecting new alternatives. The management

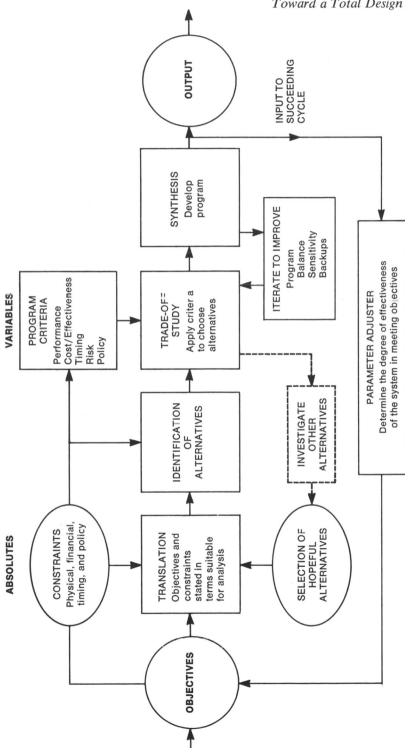

Fig. 1. STEPS WITHIN SYSTEMS APPROACH

and administration function needs to view its success in terms of the initial objectives enumerated, including an estimate of the degree to which objectives are realized and the appropriateness of the objectives themselves.

*Component analysis.* Selecting people, materials, and facilities potentially capable of accomplishing specified functions constitutes a component analysis. The results of a functional analysis form the first step of a component analysis. Alternatives potentially capable of carrying out each specified function must be identified in a component analysis and then are viewed in terms of their chances for success and their costs. Choosing components that have the highest probability for success is always desirable. Unfortunately, the painful block is frequently cost, but this is not always the case. Sometimes it is found that highly sophisticated and expensive components can be replaced with unsophisticated, inexpensive ways and means. A computer should not be programmed like a workbook when the workbook itself can serve the same purpose. One should never take a component for granted simply because it has traditionally existed; in the same sense, one should never choose an alternative because it is fashionable. Successful and productive component analyses involve the identification of alternatives that can be studied, empirically tested, and implemented to best educational and financial advantage.

The installation of a computer in many school systems illustrates the costly errors that can be made without properly identifying functions and seeking components capable of accomplishing them. The computer is a tool. Properly used, it can allow the educator to perform some functions more efficiently, more intelligently, and more accurately. Because a computer does well those functions for which it is designed, many educators hurried to purchase one before determining whether the functions performed were those that were needed. Many administrators found themselves in embarrassing positions as they discovered either that the piece of equipment was not what they needed or that they were forced to generate jobs for the computer to do in order to justify its cost. How many teaching machines have been purchased in the same manner?

Personnel must also be selected because they can function in identified ways. Personnel employed for political reasons rather than for specific competencies needed for a particular program must frequently make a job for themselves. This business of making oneself indispensable has been practiced in schools much more than either the system or individuals would like to believe. Little conclusive research exists which indicates that educational programs are either enhanced or handicapped by the presence or absence of "key" personnel. This supports the assumption that many components in the educational system do not function in a way that clearly contributes to the objectives of the system.

Adequate exploitation of a totally integrated approach to the educational enterprise dictates the emergence of new organizational patterns to facilitate doing old jobs in new ways, to eliminate some jobs, and to establish ways and means to perform completely new tasks. The new designs and operational constraints imposed by an empirically derived system cannot be tossed out because somebody subjectively condemns the system, but must be judged in relation to the ability of the system to facilitate learners in attaining educational objectives. The system is thus guarded from self-interest as well as from the pressure of special interest groups.

Establishing relationships between functions and components and constructing logical sequences are facilitated by flow charting. Procedural steps such as (1) objectifying, (2) translating, (3) analyzing, (4) selecting (trade-off), and (5) synthesizing suggest logical clusters of functions and needed components. Systems should realistically account for variables they cannot control (physical restrictions, finances, timing, policy) as well as those they can (content, performance, strategies, media, personnel).

The purpose of this discussion is not to advocate some ideal relationship that should exist in an educational system. Rather, the materials are developed in order to illustrate how functions may work together and be represented in processes and organizational configurations. The actual processes and organizations will vary from situation to situation; the principles utilized are broadly applicable to all situations. First, the functions of an educational system must be established. Second, the functions should be grouped in related clusters. Third, clusters of activities should be related in a logical way (flow chart). Fourth, men and materials should be selected because of their obvious ability to execute the functions identified.

### CHANGES IN THE EDUCATIONAL SYSTEM AND THE SUPRASYSTEM

One of the tremendous blocks to the current aims of education is that the organization functions to resist changes in society rather than to respond swiftly to the changing needs of a dynamic technological society. Many believe that this inability to change will strangle public education in the near future. Schools and their media programs must be where the action *is* if they are to have a hand in shaping the future. Most of our effort today, so the critics say, is where the action *was*.

If schools are to facilitate learning and if learning is an individual process, then the emerging role of the media specialist managing a modern educational media program must be central to any new design. Teaching and learning materials with their accompanying technologies must be a part of the main stream of the curriculum. Unfortunately such unification does not always exist. Learning materials such as films, filmstrips, educational games, and programs of instruction are left as educational subsystems of their own that are usually independent of the system of instruction conceived by an individual teacher. Media such as television, magazines, newspapers, and current films keep students instantly informed and constantly aware of reality. Strange as it may seem, these most valuable windows to the real world are blocked by many teachers or, when they are encouraged, treated as a separate exercise and rarely related to the so-called "real curriculum."

The media specialist and other media professionals are not contributing to the total instructional program when such materials as films, educational games, and magazines function as independent systems apart from the identified learning objectives. This phenomenon occurs for a number of reasons. The fact that many media specialists protect collections from students rather than make materials available for instructional needs is one point of concern. This point may be overworked. Probably teachers are also at fault. Media are too frequently identified after a system is designed for attaining specific objectives and, therefore, become a nice extra rather than an indispensible component in the total instructional program. Systems that are developed to facilitate learning could become better integrated if media specialists were involved in curriculum planning and development.

## PROPER UTILIZATION OF FEEDBACK

At one point the term *evaluation* was considered an all inclusive look at a total program, and the term *quality control* was restricted to the acceptance or rejection of manufactured goods. Today the concepts of quality control and quality verification are almost synonymous with evaluation of outcomes. Both quality control and evaluation involve procedures for obtaining, processing, and summarizing information for the purpose of judging alternative ways and means for improving a system's output (parameter adjuster).

Feedback (information) collected for the purpose of redirecting a succeeding action cycle is called quality control. The purpose, therefore, of the installation of a procedure for quality control is not to reject a product but to correct the process which in turn will modify the product. Information gained for the purpose of improving the ability of an educational media program to meet specifications is used to identify changes needed in the program. Discrepancies between intent and outcome identify the need. Adjustment occurs in the specification of objectives, the process used for attaining objectives, and/or the procedures applied for assessing outcomes.

The evaluation of a school media program requires continual monitoring. Information gained should describe the degree to which the media program is realizing its objectives. In addition, an analysis of the information should provide insight into ways and means for improvement. The utilization of feedback must be protected to insure that information gained is used for program improvement rather than for political manipulation of personnel and monies. The danger, in addition to political manipulation, is the failure to take a truly functional approach. Schools have shown the tendency to eliminate ineffective media programs and other methods for implementing the curriculum, rather than analyze why the program is not functioning in the desired manner and as a result alter it so it is congruent with the intent.

Quality control and accountability go hand in hand. The perpetual process of self-adjustment which enables media programs to become more relevant, efficient, and effective is a cycle which assists decision making. The four basic components of a quality control mechanism are:

1. an operating plan which specifies the mission in terms of criterion performance
2. an information acquisition system to determine on a timely and accurate basis the current status of the school media program
3. a system for comparing measures of effectiveness with criteria
4. a parameter adjuster to determine the processes and procedures for a succeeding action cycle.[2]

### Implications for the Media Program

1. Media specialists must be constantly aware that they function in the context of the total educational program; they must respond creatively and sensitively to the everchanging curriculum. In order to increase their ability to respond, they must assimilate and utilize information from

[2] Joe H. Mize, Charles R. White, and George H. Brooks, *Operations Planning and Control* (Englewood Cliffs, N.J.: Prentice-Hall, 1971), p. 5.

many sources. Concepts of general systems theory help bring together characteristics of all systems and provide process and structure for the application of information for the purpose of descriptive analysis.

2. The quality of functional and component analyses is related to the quality, appropriateness, and comprehensiveness of the information collected as well as to the ability to translate the information into logical task clusters.

3. In order to make a long range plan for a media program, a description of the existing program must be compared to a standard, a model of what the media program is to become. If media specialists do not know where they are going, more than likely they will never get there. The comparison of what exists with what is desired is called a discrepancy analysis. The mechanism put into action in order to systematically change the function is called a parameter adjuster.

4. Media specialists must utilize information as well as the intuition gained through experience to identify needs, alternatives, strategies, and methods for introducing adjustments into the program.

5. Ways and means of collecting information by utilizing criterion measures, questionnaires, observations and interviews, inspection of records and logs, and standardized measures open communication channels among the school media program, the community, administrators, teachers, and students. Observation and interview are perhaps the most useful techniques available to media specialists for data capture. Both techniques afford media specialists the opportunity to investigate in depth impromptu situations, to assess attitudes, to clarify functions, to promote understanding, and to overcome resistance to the media program.

---

### Problems and Activities for Research and Discussion

1. Find three definitions for each of the following terms, giving complete bibliographic references. After researching each term, formulate an original definition for each.

| | |
|---|---|
| a. administration | f. general systems theory |
| b. component analysis | g. management |
| c. criterion measure | h. quality control |
| d. feedback | i. standardized measure |
| e. functional analysis | j. system analysis |

2. Many contend that the schools must learn to adapt the technology that is available to them. In a short essay, describe the people, machines, and processes which can help contribute to more technological responsibility in the schools.

3. Describe the process of translating functions into a chart illustrating the relationships between function clusters.

4. Why must a description of a specific media program be compared to a standard?

5. Defend: The best decisions are data-based.

6. Defend or refute: Media specialists are in the business of working themselves out of business.

7. Collect three instruments designed to survey school media programs and evaluate (a) the comprehensiveness and (b) the appropriateness of each instrument.

8. What are the personality characteristics that contribute to making quality observations? Document.

9. Develop a formal research paper defending the statement: Quality control and accountability go hand in hand.

10. Investigate the similarities and differences among instructional design, instructional technology, curriculum genesis, and product development. Develop your findings into a formal, documented statement.

---

**Sample Minimodule**

Formulating Purposes

PROBLEM. The functions and components necessary for the operation of a school media program must naturally grow from the identified purposes of the program. The purposes, in turn, must support the total school program. This activity permits the student to explore the similarities and differences between more comprehensive libraries and the school media program in order to establish the unique purposes of the school media program as perceived by leaders in the field. The module utilizes the experience of each student in arriving at the criterion and permits the instructor and the students to work together toward a common end. The kind of personal interaction suggested can be classified as an inductive mode of inquiry which is common to the way purposes are usually formulated.

PERFORMANCE OBJECTIVE. Utilizing two films, a minimum of three outside resources, a process for decision making, and the experience of classmates, the student will formulate a statement of purpose for a school media program.

Enabling objectives:

1. Using the *Hottest Spot in Town* (motion picture) as an information base, list seven purposes for libraries.
2. Number each purpose from one to seven with one indicating the most important purpose and seven indicating the least important purpose.
3. Form into groups of three. Using the process of consensus, rearrange the priorities in order to reflect the best thinking of the group. Retain no more than seven purposes.
4. Combine the purposes identified by each group and reorder to show objectives adopted by the total group. Combine, rewrite, and drop until you retain no more than seven.
5. Using *At the Center* (motion picture) as an information base, list seven purposes for school media centers.
6. Number each purpose from one to seven with one indicating the most important purpose and seven indicating the least important purpose.
7. Form into groups of three. Using the process of consensus, rearrange the priorities in order to reflect the best thinking of the group. Retain no more than seven. Fewer are acceptable. Rewrite if necessary.
8. Combine the purposes identified by each group and reorder to show objectives adopted by the total group.
9. Using the identified purposes for public libraries and school media centers, identify as many similarities and differences as you deem important. Combine and drop until you retain no more than seven. Rewrite if necessary.
10. Locate and list at least three other sources which attempt to describe purposes for school media programs and for public libraries.
11. Share your findings and conclusions with other members of the group. How are your purposes different from those located by other members of the group? How are they the same? Modify and formalize your statement of purpose for a school media center.

CRITERION. The completion of a statement of purpose for a school media program is the central objective of this module. Other considerations include:

1. How did this module help you determine the process by which purposes are identified?
2. What factors determine identified purposes for a given library media center?

3. List and comment on new terms you have learned and used.
4. Was the time allowed adequate?

FOLLOW-UP ACTIVITY. Outline a procedure for identifying the purposes of a school media center using personnel from the school and community.

REFERENCES

Banathy, Bela H. *Instructional Systems*. Belmont, Calif.: Fearon, 1968.
Bertalanffy, Ludwig von. *General System Theory*. New York: George Braziller, 1968.
Borg, Walter R. *Educational Research: an Introduction*. New York: David McKay, 1963.
Brix, V. H. *You Are a Computer*. New York: Emerson, 1970.
Churchman, C. West. *The Design of Inquiring Systems*. New York: Basic Books, 1971.
Craig, Robert L., and Bittel, Lester R., eds. *Training and Development Handbook*. New York: McGraw-Hill, 1967.
Daniels, Alan, and Yeates, Donald, eds. *System Analysis*. Palo Alto, Calif.: Science Research Associates, 1971.
Dougherty, Richard M., and Heinritz, Fred. J. *Scientific Management of Library Operations*. New York: Scarecrow, 1966.
Hicks, Warren, B., and Tillin, Alma M. *Developing Multi-Media Libraries*. New York: Bowker, 1970.
Lyle, Guy R. *The Administration of the College Library*. New York: H. W. Wilson, 1961.
Martin, Lowell A. *Library Response to Urban Change*. Chicago: American Library Assn., 1969.
Mesarovic, Mihajlo D., ed. *Views on General Systems Theory*. New York: John Wiley, 1964.
Mize, Joe H., White, Charles R., and Brooks, George H. *Operations Planning and Control*. Englewood Cliffs, N.J.: Prentice-Hall, 1971.
Swarthout, Charlene R. *The School Library as Part of the Instructional System*. Metuchen, N.J.: Scarecrow, 1967.
Tracey, William R. *Designing Training and Development Systems*. New York: American Management Assn., 1971.

*Who*
*Says What*
*In Which Channel*
*To Whom*
*With What Effect?*
LASSWELL

# Interface Between the School Media Program and the Curriculum

THE ABILITY of school personnel to work together to provide a facilitating environment for learners as well as to develop discrete competencies which contribute to the whole is essential to the multidisciplinary, differentiated staff approaches to modern curriculum designs. The fact that components (personnel, facilities, and materials) exist does not insure that they will interact in such a way that the goals of the system and the needs of students are realized. Analysis is difficult because the sum of the parts does not equal the whole. The relationship between the parts— the interfaces between people, materials, and processes—must be understood if a workable concept of wholeness is to be developed.

The school media program is valued as a means for students meeting curricular objectives. It is a purposeful arrangement of processes, components, and interfacings that not only respond to but also initiate, promote, and implement educational objectives. The concept of program is preferred to the more traditional idea of service, which runs the danger of continuing programs that restrict their activities to responding and only rarely initiating. Although such operations as acquisitioning, production, management, utilization, selection, and evaluation describe aspects of the school media program, these descriptors do not constitute proper organizers for relating the school media program to the school curriculum. This is not to say that activities such as production are not a part of the school media program, but rather that production per se might evolve as an entity for and of itself unless the relationships among the needs of users, the educational program, the media program, and production are working together toward mutual ends. For example, all curricula demand that some materials be purchased, that other materials be produced, and that still other materials be repackaged on a more appropriate level or in a different format. The way personnel, machines, and facilities are organized in response to this need constitutes one aspect of the media program. A room with staff, equipment, and materials may or may not constitute an appropriate responding capacity. Lead time, for example, may stop users from requesting production of needed materials. The production operation, like other operations, interfaces with functions—management and administration, design, information, consultation. The purposeful (congruent with objectives) orchestration of functions and operations is the aim of all school media programs.

The term *interface* is increasingly being employed to describe the relationships between entities in the educational program. Any time a man or machine is exchanging information an interface is established. An interface also applies to tasks: it refers to the actions that are organized to achieve objectives. Interfacing suggests the dynamic aspect of relating tasks; this point of view creates a concern for what is happening in the program. Most task descriptions suggest numerous interfaces which are easily categorized. Consequently, task analyses and competency lists imply a virtual catalog of interfacings.

Preoccupation with things and even theories can block time that could more profitably be spent on improving working relationships. The traditional preoccupation with collections development, for example, must not displace the people needed to solve the problems of interfacing. Interfacing problems arise as materials are designed, produced, acquisitioned, stored, retrieved, utilized, and evaluated. Problems also arise, of course, as students work with materials, media personnel with materials, teachers with materials, media personnel with students, media personnel with teachers, media personnel with administrators, and media personnel with parents.

INTERFACING TASK DIMENSIONS

Management and administration, design, information, and consultation functions not only support the operations of the media program but also integrate the program with the curriculum. Figure 2 illustrates the relationships between and among functions and operations. The goal of functions is to insure effective and efficient operations by establishing close internal and external functional relationships. Complete development of all four functions can be observed in advanced, well-articulated district or system school media programs where each operation tends to be tailored to individual schools. The number and kind of operations should vary in accordance with the needs of a specific school curriculum.

Operations such as maintenance, planning, and distribution will most likely occur on the district as well as the school level. Distribution, especially that associated with networking, as well as planning should be considered on both a regional and a national basis. Even though most functions tend to present a complete picture only in terms of district or even regional programs, and even though operations may vary dramatically from one school and district to another, all functions and operations must promote the objectives and therefore the needs of the educational programs they support and implement. The objectives shown in figure 2 determine each function and operation necessary for program development and implementation. Functions do not constitute a job description for any particular professional and do not appear on a table of organiza-

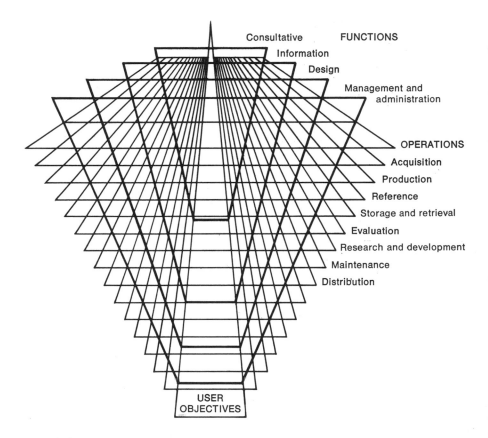

Fig. 2. MEDIA PROGRAM VIEWED AS A MESH OF INTERFACINGS

tions. They are rather a cluster of activities that must be accounted for within the media program. Available staff and needs will suggest how tasks would be divided.

*Management and administration.* The business world makes a distinction between management and administration. In this context, management develops a working philosophy, sets goals, identifies criteria, and establishes policies. Administrative duties center around carrying out the desires of management. Although this separation is useful and may guide the identification of functions in a particular institution, common practice in schools is to combine management and administration. Therefore, this discussion will consider management and administration as parts of a single decision making function which includes planning, organization, change, operation, and control as enumerated in figure 3.

Traditionally, management and administration have tended to bind both the schools and their media programs into a bureaucratic structure. In general terms, the school bureaucracy has (1) a hierarchy of authority based on a synthetic and arbitrary division of labor; (2) a standard operating procedure including rights and duties of employees; and (3) an objective, impersonal relation with employees, especially when dealing with exceptions, promotion, and change.

Management and administration have been guilty of developing each of these three entities as ends in themselves. Such practices, coupled with the school's inability to identify specific competencies associated with position titles, have created a power structure. The division of labor has been artificial rather than natural, and, consequently, power has not necessarily depended upon a specific technical competency. The development of standard operating procedure has tended toward the preservation of the institution rather than toward an increased sensitivity to the needs of school children, the community, or the employees of the district. Personnel practices and policies have been developed to prevent the institution from confronting people as people. The institution has shown little interest in mediating conflicts between individuals or in accepting and building upon the bias that exists in all humans.

In many cases the concept of a bureaucracy is in conflict with an operational democracy. The more bureaucratic, the less democratic and sensitive the institution is to the needs of the culture. Consequently, the rate of change will demand more democratic procedures, especially on the part of management. To put it another way, society's institutions must keep pace with change. Since an open system tends to be more sensitive to its environment, the trend will be toward establishing more open institutions. Bureaucratic structures tend to resist changes in many ways while democratic structures have many built-in response mechan-

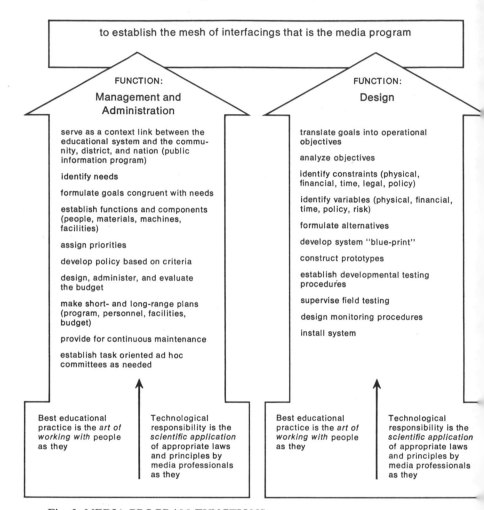

Fig. 3. MEDIA PROGRAM FUNCTIONS

isms. Democratic procedures open channels of communication with the suprasystem which, in fact, supports the institution.

Bennis and Slater account for the evolution and subsequent obsolescence of the pyramidal type bureaucracy.

Bureaucracy, as I refer to it here, is a useful social invention that was perfected during the industrial revolution to organize and direct the activities of a business firm. Most students of organizations would say that its anatomy consists of the following components: a well-defined chain of command; a system of procedures and rules for dealing with all contingencies relating to work activities; a division of labor based on specializa-

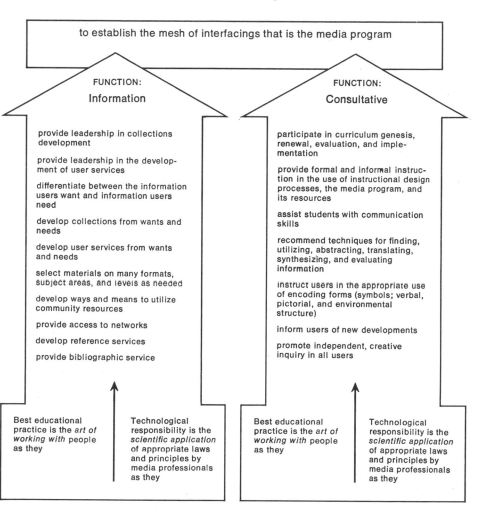

to establish the mesh of interfacings that is the media program

FUNCTION:
Information

FUNCTION:
Consultative

provide leadership in collections development

provide leadership in the development of user services

differentiate between the information users want and information users need

develop collections from wants and needs

develop user services from wants and needs

select materials on many formats, subject areas, and levels as needed

develop ways and means to utilize community resources

provide access to networks

develop reference services

provide bibliographic service

participate in curriculum genesis, renewal, evaluation, and implementation

provide formal and informal instruction in the use of instructional design processes, the media program, and its resources

assist students with communication skills

recommend techniques for finding, utilizing, abstracting, translating, synthesizing, and evaluating information

instruct users in the appropriate use of encoding forms (symbols; verbal, pictorial, and environmental structure)

inform users of new developments

promote independent, creative inquiry in all users

Best educational practice is the *art of working with* people as they

Technological responsibility is the *scientific application* of appropriate laws and principles by media professionals as they

Best educational practice is the *art of working with* people as they

Technological responsibility is the *scientific application* of appropriate laws and principles by media professionals as they

tion; promotion and selection based on technical competence; impersonality in human relations. It is the pyramid arrangement we see on most organizational charts.

The bureaucratic "machine model" was developed as a reaction against the personal subjugation, nepotism, cruelty, and the capricious and subjective judgments which passed for managerial practices during the early days of the industrial revolution. Bureaucracy emerged out of the organization's need for order and precision and the workers' demands for impartial treatment. It was an organization ideally suited to the values and demands of the Victorian era. And just as bureaucracy emerged as a creative response to a radically new age, so today new organizational shapes are surfacing before our eyes.[1]

The benevolent dictator is slowly fading from the management of our schools. The tightly run shop no longer stands proudly on its efficiency, but rather struggles defensively as the critics continually erode its foundations. Bureaucratic structures and their benevolent dictators are being replaced as more attention is given to (1) free communication on all levels, (2) consensus rather than coersion, (3) technical competency rather than organizational power, (4) task oriented structures, and (5) acceptance of human differences.[2]

Although these criticisms and trends can be applied to management and administration at all levels, the media specialist wearing his management-administrative hat has some more specific concerns. Besides the task of establishing the criteria for the organization of the media center and program, the media specialist must strive toward more scientific administration and translation of the criteria. In his leadership capacity the media specialist must attempt to develop more authentic human relations, more democratic procedures, and a more scientific posture toward the development of the school media program.

Management of personnel involves staff in setting policies related to promotion, leaves of absence, tenure, transfer and the like. The involvement of the school media staff in these and related matters insures that policies and procedures are understood and is an important method of recognizing the professional commitment of the staff. In addition, the staff should share in the decision making process of the organization.

*Design.* The design function summarized in figure 3 includes any systems approach to the solution of educational problems. The potential of systems designs can reach out to restructure the entire educational system through the planning process or be restricted to the production of a single graphic. This flexibility is due to the fact that the heart of the design function is a process, a process which can be closely associated with the scientific method. The steps of the scientific method include:

1. formulating a statement of the problem
2. collecting information
3. forming hypotheses
4. testing hypotheses
5. drawing conclusions.

[1] Warren G. Bennis and P. E. Slater, *The Temporary Society* (New York: Harper and Row, 1968), pp. 54–55.

[2] Warren G. Bennis, *Changing Organizations* (New York: McGraw-Hill, 1966), p. 19.

The parameters of the design function, as with all other functions, are determined by the kind and number of operations developed as well as by the kind and number of relationships established with other components of the media and educational programs. Each operation and function needs assistance in problems relating to design. If fully developed, the design function could be the core function of not only the school media program, but also of the total educational program.

At present, applying systems principles to the solution of all educational problems may retard the development of this function in many educational programs. Not only does this process threaten those with power, but it also runs the danger of overextending and overapplying at a time when neither personnel nor procedures exist in the kinds and numbers needed. The interest in more scientific planning and development has produced instant experts who are doing much more harm than many realize. The misuse of processes by inexperienced personnel is making the entire systems movement suspect.

At this stage of development, restricting most activities included in the design function to school media program operations seems safe. This is especially true in the area of instructional product development where people and processes appear to be more available. However, even in this area, care must be exercised in the development of instructional materials to avoid costly and complicated procedures for the sake of sophistication rather than for the benefit of the product.

In addition, a widespread state of confusion exists over such terms as systems approach, systems design, instructional design, educational technology, and instructional product development. Evidence of the confusion can easily be seen by assembling the number of definitions that exist for each term and by noting that one frequently defines another term as well. The common denominator exists in the steps to the process. All terms imply a goal-oriented procedure utilizing similar steps. The steps include translating goals into objectives, analyzing objectives, identifying constraints and variables, constructing prototypes, conducting field tests, and installing the system.

*Information.* The information function summarized in figure 3 has many dimensions and may be observed in various stages of development on several levels. For example, well developed and articulated information systems are frequently found to serve managers and administrators and, to a lesser degree, faculty members and students. Information is available to the legislative body of the school in order to justify, plan, organize, direct, change, and control the operations of the school. In many cases, such systems are integrated and computerized. The term *integrated* means that all units (administration, admissions, counseling and guidance, academic departments, schools, business office, food services) receive the information they need for operations from a central data bank. In all cases each operation is both a source and a consumer of information.

On the other hand, the student—the user of the educational system— has frequently been deprived of the type and level of information service available to the administrators, teachers, and managers of specific operations. This results in a waste of human resources as students wait in line to register, eat, visit counselors, or be assigned a textbook. In addition, students frequently need curricular materials they cannot find, or they cannot check out materials for as long as they need them, or they have to wait a specified period until materials become available. In contrast, teachers and administrators may frequently check out materials or purchase materials they want and keep them as long as they like with few questions asked about their usage.

In many cases the student should be able to command educational services much as does a consumer of a service or product. To the consumer many more options are available from a variety of stores and agencies which constantly relate consumer satisfaction to operations. Schools purporting to offer significant alternatives are frequently too far away or too expensive for students to consider seriously. In this sense schools are a kind of monopoly which can exist without much consideration for the user of the system since they have little competition. Dissatisfaction growing among students and parents could increase the service orientation of the schools. Perhaps one hope is that increased services such as telecommunications will produce a "demonstration effect" on education, forcing a more client responsive system.[3]

Students play a key role in planning and developing collections and user services. It is a natural role, for much of the business of living consists of assembling and utilizing resources needed to accomplish a task. Students need to discover as well as be told about the options that are educationally acceptable. Development of resources and user services involves careful consideration of what services are provided to whom and on what level as well as what users are expected to do for themselves.

*Consultation.* The consultation function summarized in figure 3, of the media program involves participation and leadership in curriculum development, in-service programs, and other educational activities. Curriculum responsibilities of the media program include working with teams charged with developing, renewing, evaluating, and implementing

[3] Khateeb M. Hussain, *Development of Information Systems for Education* (Englewood Cliffs, N.J.: Prentice-Hall, 1973), p. 86.

educational programs. As new curricular systems are implemented, the media program frequently organizes and conducts in-service programs to insure proper installation of the new design. Preserving the integrity of the system is necessary in order to control and estimate its value.

Effective in-service programs require a broad base of support which is best built through the creative participation of all members of the educational community. Students, teachers, administrators, and community people participate in in-service programs with greater enthusiasm when they are learning things they feel they need to know and when they work on the resolution of problems which they have helped identify. Appropriate in-service programs should be initiated from all levels in the educational community. The erroneous assumption that administrators alone can best determine and control in-service activities blocks the potential for program development and implementation. National, community, organizational, instructional, material, administrative, and content problems and resources are all possible focal points for in-service programs.

In-service programs cannot move in all directions at once. Consequently, short- and long-range planning is essential. Carefully defined objectives based on priorities for a given year should make clear the program's emphasis. For example, the thrust for a particular year may be programs designed to build respect for school and community property or to encourage creativity.

When the consultation function of the media program is fully developed, all formal in-service activities may be managed by the district and school media program. The functions, operations, and facilities of the district media program and the school media program provide the philosophical orientation and the working environment conducive to effective in-service programs. This obligation already includes informal and formal instruction in the use of design procedures, techniques of mediation, and appropriate utilization and dissemination of innovations and new materials.

### TRADITIONAL OPERATIONS

Acquisition, production, reference, storage and retrieval, evaluation and selection, research and development, maintenance, and distribution are examples of generic categories for operations that may be included in a media program.

*Acquisition.* The entire process of the acquisition of materials has but one goal. That goal is to acquire materials as quickly and inexpensively as possible. The grave danger of any isolated operation is its tendency to be self-serving. Some acquisition procedures are classic examples of accountability standing in the road of accessibility. Simple orders may entail hours of paper work on numerous levels when a simple phone call might solve the problem. Rigorous screening and approval procedures can delay an order for weeks. Holding orders and writing elaborate justification for materials slow the acquisition process. Whenever procedures can be simplified in order to gain speed and to cut costs, they should be carefully studied and implemented if at all possible. Careful study could imply another roadblock. Studies should not be made for the sake of studies nor should they be employed as a device to slow down changes that are long overdue.

The general thrust of the objectives outlined by Melcher on acquiring book materials applies to many materials.

> Find a way to buy service instead of discount. The great majority of libraries of all types have long since won their freedom from blind acceptance of the low bid. You can, too. You must.
> Encumber only upon receipt. If necessary, have an agreement in writing with the supplier that all his shipments are "on approval" until paid for, though you do not expect to take advantage of this.
> Pay on the supplier's invoice, ask no special billing.
> Pay promptly. Pay for partial shipments. Pay invoices as rendered; spot-check their accuracy later. If you are dealing with a reputable supplier, you can be sure he won't hesitate to rectify errors found later.
> Order often. Don't keep your readers waiting. An order of 50 to 100 books is not too small.
> Simplify your paper work. Make one writing meet all needs. Order by slip, not list. Have no more than five parts to your form set.
> Get what you order. Enforce your contracts. Spot-check performance.
> Know your inside costs. Let your supplier do anything he can do cheaper.[4]

An incredible number of routines for the procurement of materials exists for no particular reason or for administrative convenience. Bureaucratic structures and red tape too quickly subvert and make docile both media specialist and users. A point of amazement centers around how faculty quickly reconcile themselves to the fact that materials ordered one year will not arrive until the next. The specification of needs and criteria by key administrative and purchasing personnel can help screen out unnecessary procedures and speed up acquisition.

*Production.* Production can range from the development of a simple transparency to a package involving the whole process of product development—designing, producing prototypes, validating, and installing the product in its appropriate setting. In some cases production opera-

---

[4] Daniel Melcher, *Melcher on Acquisition* (Chicago: American Library Assn., 1971), p. 3.

tions mean almost the same thing as the design function herein described.

The production operation in school library media centers may be providing a room where teachers prepare their own materials, a media center where materials and machines provide a workshop for both students and teachers, or a complete production center staffed by photographers, graphic artists, instructional designers, programmers, and other professionals. Personnel working in production departments frequently must provide training for students and teachers, write programs and scripts for visual presentations, make original drawings for various visuals, record and narrate, and in some cases even build prototypes and facilities. Production departments in school media centers may include the reproduction of materials by spirit processes, mimeograph, offset, XEROX, Gestefax, and other commonly used duplicating methods.

Because of the wide variety of activities that can be generally considered as production, school media centers may label aspects of their programs in any number of ways. In highly advanced media programs, specialists actually serve as consultants in the teaching and learning process when they engage in the designing of specific materials and programs of instruction. Schools possessing this capability may prefer such designations as the "department of instructional development" or the "department of curriculum development." At any rate the impact of the fields of instructional technology and communication theory have completely transformed the old idea of production into a vital process which, when fully developed, may be a separate function (design).

Designing instructional materials according to curricular specifications utilizes principles and practices of instructional technology and communication theory. General theoretical knowledge about the target population, best educational practice, and the potential of man-machine systems (technological responsibility) is necessary in order to design instructional materials. Developers of instructional materials must understand and apply principles of motivation, readiness, reinforcement, cueing, pacing, sequencing, and retention to production problems. In addition, the instructional designer needs to be able to analyze and describe the subject matter he is working with in terms of principles, hierarchies, supporting facts, and so forth. Being able to translate broad objectives into behavioral objectives, sequencing learning tasks, selecting appropriate strategies, matching media to the communication tasks, designing criterion measures, and building prototypes may all be considered production tasks in a media program.

*Reference.* Although the purpose of reference services is clear, the school media setting is frequently not developed to the point that reference services can operate in the same manner as a large research or public library. The basic reason for looking at reference as a separate operation is to draw attention to the part information services play in the school media program. The center should be able to provide the information requested by its users, a purpose which requires a reference service as comprehensive as the recorded knowledge of all mankind. The difficulty of providing reference services in the school not only relates to the limited collections that are available, but also to the increased sophistication of the requests due to the impact of mass media. Consequently, the completeness of the reference service provided by any school media specialist usually must rely upon an ability to unite and articulate the school media program with other sources of information within the community and through available district and regional programs and networks. In other words, reference services, in many cases, become referral services. The media specialist must also learn to distinguish between reference questions arising from the need for information itself and those stemming from the need to learn to use informational resources such as indexes.

What students ask for and what they want may be two quite different things. Consequently the school media specialist must learn to ask questions skillfully in order to help students specify and refine their requests. The tradition of teaching students to retrieve information for themselves is erroneously thought of as reference service. Students need and have the right to obtain information upon request just as professionals do when they ask for information at the local public library.

Negotiating reference questions and using the information sources of the community and available networks are skills that must be developed and nurtured if reference services are to fulfill their critical roles. First, if students encounter positive responses early and consistently, they will more than likely continue to patronize and support the services. Second, reference services bring the media specialist and students into face-to-face contact. This relationship is extremely important for the formation of positive attitudes toward the media program.

Reference services demand a knowledge about as much content and as many sources of information as possible. Generally speaking, skills that are associated with reference work include:

1. question negotiations
2. classification of the question
3. search strategy
4. delivery of appropriate information in terms of the user.[5]

[5] William A. Katz, *Introduction to Reference Work, Vol. 1: Basic Information Sources* (New York: McGraw-Hill, 1969), p. 3.

*Storage and retrieval.* Systems for storage and retrieval of media include the classification of all information sources. Most centers need to follow closely a specific classification system which may include subject headings, descriptive catalogs, card catalogs, computer book catalogs, and shelf lists. The primary concerns of media personnel in the area of storage and retrieval are accurate identification and easy access. It is generally agreed that the main access point, whether it be a card or book catalog, enables a person to identify a book, filmstrip, film, study print, or other material by its author, title, or subject. After a specific material is located in the catalog or list, the user must know its physical location.

The great variation between centralized and decentralized collections should relate to the differences among school programs. Although centralization of materials can result in better management and more efficient and economical services from the standpoint of maximum use of a minimum number of materials, centralization incompatible with the needs of the educational program may be a block rather than a facilitator. Regardless of whether materials are centralized or decentralized, the critical point usually rests with whether or not the system has made available to the student and teacher the materials they need when they need them. Rational organization is essential. A justification must tie the classification and organization of materials to the needs of the educational program. In the broadest sense, there is not a best way of storing and retrieving materials. There are only appropriate ways given the constraints and demands of a particular school or district.

Unfortunately, for the media specialist, the best system for any school or educational program demands a thorough knowledge of the alternative methods of classification and retrieval available. This means that the media specialist must know not only the general principles of cataloging which include basic rules but also the potential of color codes, symbols, formats, index reproduction systems, and so on. The whole process of storage and retrieval frequently looms as an impossible task to the media specialist. Nevertheless, accessibility of materials to users depends to a large part upon the efficient storage and retrieval systems of any particular center.

*Evaluation and selection.* The evaluation and selection of educational material is, perhaps, the most difficult of all operations because of the ambiguity that surrounds perceived needs. Most often the search centers around some materials which relate to some general curriculum area. When students and teachers desire a specific material, in a particular format, on a specific level, and in a narrowly defined content area, the chances are that the material is not commercially available. Because generalized, "balanced" collections have not functioned as well as they might and because specific materials are unavailable, the media specialist and others concerned with the evaluation and selection of materials find themselves in a frustrating, awkward situation. Perhaps this is why materials selection committees have long entertained themselves with forms and checklists remarkably void of the most critical questions.

*Research and development.* As curriculum development and instructional product development merge as one and as the school media program becomes an integral part of the educational program by design, research and development become more important in the total school program. In a sense the schools are moving toward a more scientific approach (toward more technological responsibility) in all their endeavors. Selecting variables for research and development, finding and interpreting educational research studies, designing experimental and research activities, and interpreting studies are all becoming more prominent in schools today. Whether or not a formal research and development component exists in a particular school is, perhaps, not as important as the change in attitude of personnel concerned with generating, producing, and evaluating the efforts of the schools. As more promising organizational configurations are formulated and tested, and as the means and the ends of curricula become more congruent, the role of research and development will become more important.

*Maintenance.* Maintenance becomes a complex process in well developed media programs if materials and equipment are kept in good condition and ready for use. Minor repairs such as reinforcing materials, changing bulbs and fuses, repairing cords, and cleaning and adjusting equipment are most appropriately performed at the site of usage which, in most cases, is the school. All other repairs and reconditioning are usually managed by the district media equipment shop. Pools of adequate equipment and materials are necessary to maintain operational levels when equipment is being repaired or when materials such as periodicals are in the bindery.

Materials and equipment are replaced when maintenance costs become excessive. Although preventive maintenance will result in a longer life of both materials and equipment, replacing and updating on a regularly scheduled basis must be a part of the master plan, too. These needs should be reflected in the budget.

*Distribution.* Distribution systems such as the delivery and pickup of films, displays, machines, and materials are necessary if the district services and collections are to be utilized by the individual schools and if the schools are able to exchange machines and materials on any regular basis. Distribution may make use of trucks assigned to the media program, the federal mail service, and other delivery services, personally owned automobiles, student messengers, or other means. Most important are schedules, equipment, and personnel to provide the services and machines and materials that support the educational programs.

*Technical processing and collections development.* The concepts of technical processing and collections development are broad areas that include several operations. Technical processing includes acquisition, processing of materials, and cataloging. Concepts which center around collections development are more difficult to define. Generally speaking, a philosophy for developing collections is included as a guide for developing selection criteria. Ways and means of both selecting materials and assuring that the collection is congruent with the curriculum are also important elements. Setting the parameters for the depth and breadth of a collection again necessitates the establishment of criteria. What operations are named is not as important as whether or not they account for the needs of the program. Far too many professionals are being trained in specific techniques for selecting fiction, nonfiction, government documents, pamphlets, filmstrips, microforms, films, realia kits, slides, transparencies, and other items without an adequate concept of the projected need for resources for any given program. In other words, professionals are being trained to apply criteria for each medium and genre but are not working with students, teachers, and the curriculum to the extent they should.

### IDENTIFYING INTERFACES

Most personnel are aware that media programs must accommodate advanced, reliable, and replicatable systems of instruction as well as relate to the self-contained classroom, mini-courses, and other activities that integrate media center usage with the curriculum. Practically every configuration of media program components can be found in existence somewhere as a result of the tremendous number of curriculum designs and an equally astounding number of logistical problems.

Three elements generally exist in any attempt to identify interfaces. First, the status quo is ascertained, usually through a kind of task analysis. Second, expert opinion is solicited and used to add, delete, and modify the tasks listed. Third, some objective mechanical process is applied to establish priorities. The director of the School Library Manpower Project (SLMP) provided school library supervisors in fifty state departments of education with a "Criteria of Excellence Checklist" in order to identify exemplary programs. The project then contracted with the Research Division of the National Education Association to conduct a task analysis survey in the schools selected. This survey concentrated on exemplars.

> The use of this special type of sample was fundamental to the purposes of the study: The identification of the best in school library media centers, the types of personnel staffing those centers, and the tasks performed by persons in each type of position. The best, thus, becomes a benchmark in the development of relevant training programs for library media center staff positions.[6]

The project enlisted the help of experts in the development of three hundred task statements. The computer was used to group the tasks identified into twelve major categories:

1. development of educational program
2. administration
3. instruction
4. special services to faculty and students
5. selection
6. acquisition
7. production
8. preparation of materials
9. organization
10. circulation
11. maintenance
12. clerical and secretarial tasks.[7]

The actual tasks identified give the first clue to the important concept of interfacing. For example, in relation to the development of the educational program, SLMP lists thirteen tasks:

1. Participates in curriculum development and revision
2. Assists curriculum committees in selection of appropriate materials for resource units and curriculum guides
3. Assists individual teachers in curriculum planning
4. Conducts evaluation of adequacy and suitability of facilities, equipment, materials, and services with regard to learning outcomes
5. Provides leadership in determining educational objectives of library services

---

[6] School Library Manpower Project, *School Library Personnel Task Analysis Survey* (Chicago: American Association of School Librarians, 1969), p. 7.
[7] Ibid., pp. 10–11, 20.

6. Develops long-range plan cooperatively with faculty and administration
7. Plans cooperatively with faculty members to coordinate materials and library activities with curriculum programs, units, and textbooks
8. Observes classroom work to coordinate library activities with school instructional programs
9. Participates in team-teaching activities
10. Plans and discusses library-involved topics, units, and activities with teachers
11. Develops new uses for materials and equipment
12. Engages in research activities relative to educational media and media center programs
13. Works with teachers to design innovations in instruction.[8]

Each of these tasks employs the interfaces necessary for fully functional programs. The problem that arises is that specific tasks identified under each of the above headings as well as under the other twelve subject headings may be infinitely complex. For example, Task Number Three, "assists individual teachers in curriculum planning," can be interpreted as involving implementation of teachers' plans on a one-to-one basis or as requiring participation in the design and development of programs. Nevertheless, the interfaces established between media specialists and teachers as well as between media specialists and students in the process of curriculum planning are crucial for quality programs. These interfaces mean working with, not merely assisting or simply doing what one is told to do.

An even better resource for identifying interfacings is SLMP's *Behavioral Requirements Analysis Checklist* of performance standards for school library media specialists. Approximately seven hundred tasks are organized under seven areas—human behavior, learning and learning environment, planning and evaluation, media, management, research, and professionalism.[9]

All interfaces have at least two common elements. First, a rapport must exist between the two entities whether they are people or man-machine systems. Second, one has to contribute to the goals of the other. Again, in the case of the task which brings media specialists into the curriculum planning process, the media specialist must not only establish a good working relationship but must also be able to make a contribution.

[8] Ibid., p. 22.
[9] School Library Manpower Project, *Behavioral Requirements Analysis Checklist* (Chicago: American Library Assn., 1973).

If interfacing is to be effective, attendant skills must be involved. Let us consider interfacing with students. After a good working relationship is established, the media specialist must know and be able to apply physical, mental, emotional, and social processes as they relate to, for example, motivation, readiness, reinforcement, cueing, pacing, sequencing, and retention.

Both encouraging the self-initiated interests of students and attracting them to activities they might otherwise avoid or overlook can be described as *motivation*. The media specialist helps students strive toward a balance between interests and requirements and encourages students to extend their attention and interests. Since most students are motivated by involvement and discovery, media programs should encourage activities that require participation and experimentation. Highly motivated individuals generally possess two desirable characteristics. First, they are overachievers; second, they experience satisfaction. Unless students experience satisfaction in school experiences, they will show signs of apathy and decrease their efforts. Media specialists have a clear responsibility to assist users in such a way that they will develop initiative and enjoy personal achievement. However, lack of motivation must not be confused with lack of readiness.

The fact that certain kinds of learning occur more readily and easily at one developmental stage than at another and in one environment than in another can be accounted for by *readiness*. The assumption is that conditions of readiness can be brought about by the management of the external environment if the developmental level of the learner is taken into account. Conditions of readiness are controlled to a large degree by prerequisite experiences which affect what a student can learn at any given stage of development and under what conditions (environments). Both external and internal reinforcement can also play an important role in developing conditions of readiness. Readiness in the cognitive domain seems to be closely related to the learner's ability to conceptualize the learning task. The most important principle regarding readiness is that "the risks of delaying instruction too long seem much less than the possible disadvantages of forcing instruction on a child who is still far from his optimal readiness for the subject of instruction."[10] Forcing instruction frequently alienates learners from gaining skills necessary for functioning well in the culture. Mathematics and English usage are classic examples. Reinforcement techniques can also play an important role in a student's acceptance or rejection of a course of study.

[10] Arthur R. Jensen, "Understanding Readiness: An Occasional Paper," *Challenge* 1:6 (Nov./Dec. 1972).

The act of encouraging desirable behavior for the purposes of motivation and retention is called *reinforcement*. Media specialists should focus on finding desirable traits to encourage rather than concentrate on inappropriate behavior. In some instances the process of disciplining students provides reinforcement for actions the media specialist may hope to discourage. Another danger is to assume that an adequate number of appropriate reinforcers are in the environment. A better posture is built when the media program responds by planning curriculum related activities that provide for recognized success experiences. For example, when the media specialist knows that a group of children are going to visit a center to find out about Eskimos, people and materials should be arranged to provide access to information as individual interests develop and to evoke curiosity.

To reinforce and encourage students in many positive ways *cueing* techniques can be utilized. Cueing is the signal (stimulus) that elicits a response. The master teacher can use questioning techniques as cues which lead the student toward discovery and cause the student to view content in different ways. For example, a simple context cue, "life has changed, is changing, and will _____," may involve students in forming a basic biological principle. In practice, cueing is frequently a kind of structured dialogue which produces student involvement and discovery. Regardless of the kind of cue utilized, whether in formal programmed instruction or in the day-to-day, face-to-face contact teachers have with learners, knowing the individual learner is essential to developing effective cueing techniques. A simple gesture can be an effective cue if the two individuals communicating know each other well. Cueing is more difficult and less subtle if the teacher and the student are of different subcultures because they lack the many ways of exchanging information which are indicative of each group. Applying principles of cueing as well as motivation, readiness, and reinforcement increases the sensitivity of the media specialist to the student and to the effective-affective nature of the program.

The way instruction is paced also contributes to the quality of an educational program. *Pacing* is the time alloted to each part of an instructional sequence—a frame on a filmstrip, discussion, reading, listening, and so on. The speed of any presentation must take into consideration both the purpose of the activity and the characteristics of the audience. Time-locked forms such as motion pictures are generally not appropriate when memorization of details is demanded. Ideally, speed should stretch or tax a student's ability without passing him by. Learning sequences which are easily started, stopped, backed up, and moved forward are frequently wise choices for individualized programs.

The order in which instructional segments are built into larger units is called *sequencing*. The key to understanding a sequence is the identification of necessary prerequisite knowledge and skills. Generally the curricula of schools have both artificial and natural sequences. For example, there is good reason to learn to add, subtract, and multiply before learning to divide. However, there is little evidence to support the theory that one should, in biology, start with the cell and finish with a study of the whole organism. To many, starting with the organism and then analyzing the parts makes just as much pedagogical sense. Consequently, media specialists and teachers must be constantly looking for topics, subjects, and skills that can be learned independently, and differentiating them from learning that requires prerequisite behaviors. Generally speaking, sequencing is facilitated when precise instructional objectives are formulated. At least two routes should be designed for learners. Developmental testing will help to verify both approaches and establish sequence. After designing learning experiences to produce the desired results, education professionals should further refine the sequence for greater efficiency. Empirical testing of hopeful alternatives is the best way to determine sequence. The purpose of applying principles of motivation, readiness, reinforcement, cueing, pacing, sequencing, and retention is to help insure that learning will take place and that critical competencies will be retained.

The act of remembering is *retention*. What one knows and is able to recall at will is retained in permanent storage. Retention is reduced when too many events occur at one time, when too many distractors interfere with activities, and when too much time elapses.[11] Retention should be differentiated from activities such as scanning, perceiving, monitoring the environment, and holding something in mind for a short while. Motivation, pacing, cueing, and repetition can be structured to aid memory.

### FUNCTIONAL AND PROCESS RELATIONSHIPS

Because of the intricacy of accounting for all behaviors necessary to the identification of interfaces, some researchers employ matrix systems to guide the generation of tasks, and yet relate them to basic functional categories as shown in figure 4. Both two-dimensional and three-dimensional models can be utilized. When the interfaces between functions and people need to be analyzed, a grid can be set up with the functions along one axis and the responsibilities along the other. If "technical" is con-

---

[11] Robert M. Gagné, *The Conditions of Learning* (New York: Holt, Rinehart and Winston, 1970), p. 79.

| TASKS | FUNCTIONAL GROUPINGS | | | | | | | | |
|---|---|---|---|---|---|---|---|---|---|
| | Research and development | Evaluation | Design | Production | Logistics | Utilization | Organizational management | Information management | Personnel management |
| Directive-Administrative | 1* | 2 | 3 | 4 | 5 | 6 | 7 | 8 | 9 |
| Professional | 10 | 11 | 12 | 13 | 14 | 15 | 16 | 17 | 18 |
| Artistic-Production | 19 | 20 | 21 | 22 | 23 | 24 | 25 | 26 | 27 |
| Technical | 28 | 29 | 30 | 31 | 32 | 33 | 34 | 35 | 36 |
| Clerical | 37 | 38 | 39 | 40 | 41 | 42 | 43 | 44 | 45 |
| Manual | 46 | 47 | 48 | 49 | 50 | 51 | 52 | 53 | 54 |

SOURCE: Adapted from Dale G. Hamreus, ed., *Media Guidelines: Development in Validation of Criteria for Evaluating Media Training* (Washington, D.C.: Bureau of Research, Office of Education, U.S. Dept. of Health, Education, and Welfare, June, 1970), p. III–3.

* Numbers in cells refer to particular task clusters listed in source.

Fig. 4. RESPONSIBILITY GROUPINGS BY FUNCTIONS MATRIX

sidered to be a kind of responsibility and "production" a function, then the interface can be analyzed apart from other interfaces in the matrix. The technical-production interface would consist of people-people, machine-machine, and people-machine. Again, these interfaces are more easily seen when tasks are identified.

Some researchers equate operations and functions and have compared them to the responsibilities of personnel. For example, of the 158 tasks listed by Dale Hamreus under technical-production, only 8 could be categorized as people-people interfacings.[12] The remaining 150 tasks would be more properly categorized as people-machine, people-materials, and people-process interfacings. Even though there are some 150 tasks such as "sets up machinery," "shoots film," "threads film in developing tank reel," and "mixes chemicals," the 8 interfacings that may be classified as people-people are infinitely more complex. In other words, the technical aspects seem to have been analyzed in careful detail

[12] Dale G. Hamreus, ed., *Media Guidelines: Development in Validation of Criteria for Evaluating Media Training* (Washington, D.C.: Bureau of Research, Office of Education, U.S. Dept. of Health, Education, and Welfare, June, 1970), pp. III–69— III–75.

whereas the interpersonal aspects tend to have been treated as exaggerated statements. Tasks that required people-people interfaces included:

1. discusses features of needed equipment with chief engineer
2. teaches operation of new equipment to operator
3. confers with chief engineer and others on overall plans of expansion of facilities, integration of new equipment or improvement procedures and capability
4. directs floor crew in arranging set according to director's sketch
5. relays director's instructions to the talent
6. serves as inter-personal relations coordinator by putting guest talent at ease, assuring cooperation among crew members, and acts as liaison between director and floor personnel
7. cuts from camera to camera in response to the director's commands
8. works in close teamwork with director.[13]

Similarly, three-dimensional models such as figure 5 may be developed in order to isolate interfaces. A logical model might incorporate the context (setting or environment), people (media specialist, technician, administrator), and operations (reference, productions, selection). In the case of a three-dimensional model, each cell would be numbered and studied separately.

Attempts to identify and improve contacts such as the interfacing of the teacher and the learner with media are essential to media program development. The continuing search for organizers allows media professionals to identify critical interfaces. The literature suggests many kinds of organizers which have the potential of identifying interfaces that can help stretch the role of media and other education professions. The concept of the media specialist as the mediator between the user and the universe of stored information is an example of one such organizer. Indeed, the media specialist and other professionals may also be viewed as facilitators to the teaching-learning process; as diagnosticians who can recognize what students need and suggest a suitable prescription; as arbitrators; as negotiators; and as innovators.

Media specialists and other personnel who are looking for a published list of purposes, functions, and essential interfaces which will meet their specific needs are naive. Understanding wholeness, the mesh of interfacings, lies in the identification of the relationships between the entities. Since personnel and operations differ from program to program, each program must identify relationships for itself. The identification of interfaces among people, machines, materials, and processes then becomes part of the process of developing an educational program.

[13] Ibid.

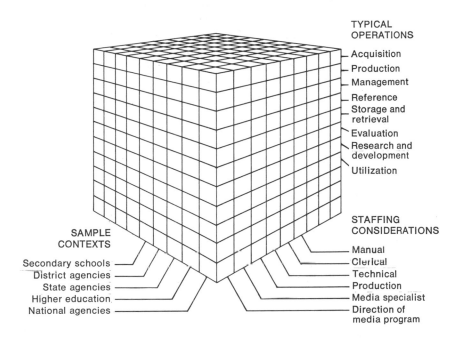

TYPICAL
OPERATIONS

Acquisition
Production
Management
Reference
Storage and
retrieval
Evaluation
Research and
development
Utilization

SAMPLE
CONTEXTS

STAFFING
CONSIDERATIONS

Secondary schools
District agencies
State agencies
Higher education
National agencies

Manual
Clerical
Technical
Production
Media specialist
Direction of
media program

Fig. 5. INTERFACINGS AMONG CONTEXTS, STAFFING,
AND OPERATIONS

In summary, the ability of school personnel to develop effective working relationships and to contribute specific competencies is critical to the building of quality programs. The social context is demanding a more unified, holistic approach to the total educational endeavor. Identifying the interfaces between components in the educational program is just as essential as identifying the components themselves. This process must be done in context and will differ from one educational setting to the next for at least two reasons. First, the context changes from one community to the other. Second, the needs and, consequently, the purposes will differ from community to community. The overarching interfaces are effective interpersonal relationships and effective machine and material usage.

### CHANGING INTERFACES

Recognizing changing interfaces is as important as labeling those that may be observed in current practice. Maintaining appropriate interfacings in such a rapidly changing technological society is a constant struggle. For example, the invention of programmed texts has demanded a different relationship between the student and the material. Teaching students to utilize programmed material is merely keeping up with the times. The adjustments made by families for television is a similar kind of change.

These kinds of changing interfaces are not jumping ahead but rather closing the gap. Anticipating and developing new relationships is infinitely more difficult, yet more necessary than simply responding. For example, the ability of a media specialist to diagnose learning problems and to suggest appropriate learning materials and strategies to users is badly needed yet largely undeveloped both in theory and in practice.

Contemplating the potential of print as well as of new technologies such as telecommunications and networking staggers the imagination. There are so many ways to learn, to receive information, and to send messages that it is difficult to explore all possible interfacings. However, in order to establish a completely compatible man-machine interface, all possibilities must be thoroughly explored. The oneness that a man feels when driving his automobile (man-machine system) is an example of this state. Curling up in a comfortable chair with a good book is another example. Much practice and creative exploration are necessary to establish the rapport that facilitates maximum information exchange. The student must work with many kinds of programmed materials before he can understand their potential; likewise, one must practice and experiment over an extended period of time before becoming completely familiar with all of the things that a particular camera can do.

Sitting back and waiting to see what the media can do is a passive response. Rather, users should analyze what they can do with media. Those who expect the media to entertain and to do the work cannot possibly develop the interface necessary for maximum information exchange. Far too much time and energy are spent in arguing and in theorizing about the potential value of media mixes rather than in establishing the many interfaces that await discovery. Format, ease of machine operation, fidelity of sound, and sequencing of messages are examples of conditions that are juggled in order to produce maximum capability.

The student-machine-material interfaces develop naturally from the abundant curiosity of the young. Media specialists, on the other hand, may have a more difficult time establishing rapport with the machine or material because they are apt to jump too fast to evaluating and not spend enough time in experimenting. The child's response may in many instances be a better indicator of the value of a media-mix than the studied opinion of the certified expert.

NEEDS ASSESSMENT AND SCHOOL MEDIA PROGRAM PLANNING

The purpose of a needs assessment is to facilitate the development of an educational program more responsive to the community and society and of a media program more responsive to the needs of the educational program. A needs assessment identifies discrepancies between the product of a system and what the larger system expects. In an educational system, the product is behavior change in students. Needs assessments are part of program planning and are distinguished from a discrepancy evaluation designed to test the efficiency and effectiveness of a unit of instruction. Needs assessments are used to determine a system's purpose and to identify outcomes to be modified, added, and/or deleted. They provide information concerning priorities that must be utilized in building budgets.

A needs assessment per se does not include the processes whereby ends are achieved or the mechanism by which objectives are adjusted to better fill the needs of the suprasystem. Rather, a needs assessment provides a process to identify and rank changes to be made in order for the educational program to adjust to the expectations of the public it serves. In the same way, the media program makes a needs assessment in order to identify changes that need to be made.

Isolating the concerns users have is the first major problem in assessing needs of the media program. The questions educators ask of representative populations will control the kind of information they receive. The value of any needs assessment depends upon whether or not the most critical questions are isolated for development into statements of need. Students, parents, community members, consultants, and educators assist in identifying critical questions which relate to the media program. These persons reduce the risk of the needs assessment addressing biased sets of questions. In addition, it is important that the initial set of questions express the concerns with utmost candor and clarity.

A needs assessment of the media program will use a different proportion of the population identified—students, parents, community members, consultants, and educators—than would a needs assessment for the total educational program. Since the educational program is the primary context of the media program, the majority of members serving as information resources for a needs assessment of the media program forms a representative body of the educational program. In other words, the greatest proportion of people involved should come directly from the most immediate context or suprasystem.

Some argue that a school media program should wait to make a needs assessment after the educational program has completed such an assessment. All media programs benefit from a greater understanding and articulation of the needs of users as they relate to educational programs. Media program planners must learn to live with the fact that educational programs are dynamic, and that any needs assessment is a questionable, tentative, and continuous process.

One particularly frustrating argument is that increasing the effectiveness of a particular media program may be assisting the educational system in advancing programs the educational system should not have in the first place. Also, systems changed to respond to one need sometimes create other problems. For example, opening up the media center may be an invitation for some teachers to send troublesome students to the center in order to stop them from disrupting the classroom. Developing and making readily accessible a rich and varied film collection may result in some teachers using films unscrupulously and extensively for the purpose of buying time rather than for moving forward the educational program. Although media personnel cannot overlook the misuse of increased opportunities, media program planners cannot use these kinds of situations as excuses for maintaining closed, tightly controlled media programs.

The inclusion of representatives from the total educational program in a process for identifying needs provides a potentially balanced viewpoint. In addition, carefully planned representation reduces the criticism of outcomes and offers firmer support for program priorities. Collective representation also provides an information function in that participants invariably develop a greater understanding of the potential and actual impact of the media program as it functions as part of the educational program. These representatives become a coordinating committee.

Three levels of needs assessment should be considered for any media program. The first level includes the on-line assessment of media personnel as they interact with users. This level includes the attitude on the part of media personnel that invites comments and open discussion of user needs. Visitations of media professionals in classes, department meetings, and curriculum planning meetings can be part of an on-line needs assessment. This level also includes devices such as suggestion boxes and impromptu questionnaires. An open door policy on the part of media professionals also encourages users to offer comments and suggestions when concerns arise. However, this policy should incorporate a visible process for action as users should know how needs and suggestions are acted upon and that the process is real and functional. Table 1 is a display of the process of on-line assessment.

Concentrating on developing areas of the curriculum constitutes the second level of needs assessment. This level may be in response to the development and installation of a new program of studies in a subject area or a change in the implementation of an established program. Level two involves the development of curriculum given a high priority by the building and district educational program. Currently, programs relating to career education could fit into this category. If there are no high priority areas established by the educational program, the media program should initiate plans for an in-depth analysis of various service areas. In other words, the media program creates long-range plans that specify a series of targets for in-depth needs assessment to be conducted during a given year.

The third level of needs assessment identifies program goals and general operational guidelines. For example, priorities may be given for a specified time to the development of a competency-based social studies program. This level sets priorities in response to the total educational program and produces a set of goals that are translated into general policy and overall functions. Each level seeks to (1) identify the questions it needs to ask, (2) collect information bearing on those questions, and (3) establish priorities. In addition, each level must establish policies and procedures, generate acceptable indicator performance, and communicate with program planners.

Each level is considered separately because each has different purposes and procedures and utilizes a different user population for the identification of needs. Level one, on-line needs assessment, makes on-the-spot identification of user needs and creates short-term targets in response to immediate concerns. Level two, in-depth needs assessment, provides an opportunity to respond to an area of the educational program which otherwise may not be included in level one or level three. Level two concentrates on the special needs of areas including student recreational collections and student productions as well as subject areas such as social studies, science, language arts, mathematics, fine arts, and physical education. Level three sets broad goals and communicates to the highest level of educational program planning. Typical considerations include merging services, separating services, creating new district and building level functions, and establishing guidelines for basic collections and facilities planning. Separating each level in this manner not only allows for more involvement on the part of the total educational community but also provides the opportunity for members to serve in ways more directly related to their primary interests. Considerations for planning a needs assessment program are summarized in figure 6.

All three levels identify discrepancies between what is expected and what is received by the user (level 1); between what support a specific curriculum needs, *e.g.,* social studies, and what it gets (level 2); and

Table 1: HYFOTHETICAL NEEDS ASSESSMENT TABLE

STUDENTS

| SAMPLE STUDENT QUESTIONS | POSSIBLE PRIORITY CONSIDERATION | SAMPLE PROCESSING INFORMATION NEEDED | RELATED MEDIA FUNCTION/ OPERATION(S) | POSSIBLE INDICATOR RESPONSES |
|---|---|---|---|---|
| Why can't students check out audio cassette recorders to work with at home? | List possible student uses. Identify potential teacher assignments requiring an audio cassette recorder. | State numbers desiring audio cassette equipment check-out service—students and teachers. Estimate existing responding capacity in view of need. Project increase in equipment, storage, and maintenance in terms of money, facilities, and personnel. | Management and administration/storage and retrieval, maintenance, distribution | Percent of change in student use of audio cassette equipment—numbers checked out and type of usage. |
| Why don't we have any materials about Eskimos? | Identify discrepancies in terms of unit needs about Eskimos. Investigate the number of teachers teaching the unit simultaneously. | List materials available. List ways and means of securing materials not in the school media center. Identify materials requested but not available. Order preview materials. Estimate costs of needed materials. State procedure for alerting teachers and students to resources available. | Consultation, information, management and administration/acquisition, production, reference, storage and retrieval, evaluation, distribution | Document frequency of utilization. State change in old and new ways of materials utilization. |

TEACHERS

| SAMPLE TEACHER QUESTIONS | POSSIBLE PRIORITY CONSIDERATION | SAMPLE PROCESSING INFORMATION NEEDED | RELATED MEDIA FUNCTION/ OPERATION(S) | POSSIBLE INDICATOR RESPONSES |
|---|---|---|---|---|
| Why does the movie projector always break down when it gets to my room? | Determine frequency of occurrence of problem. | Review maintenance program. | Management and administration/ maintenance | Percent of change in frequency of problem occurrence. |
| | | List ways and means of improving existing preventative maintenance. | | Type and degree of change in satisfaction expressed by user population. |
| | | Estimate increase in machine replacement, maintenance materials and equipment, and reconditioning costs needed to keep equipment in better running order. | | |
| How can students be stopped from copying the encyclopedia whenever they are sent to the media center to research a topic? | Document frequency of occurrence of problem. | List teachers making these kinds of assignments. | Consultation/ reference | Percent of change in number of complaints by teachers making research assignments. |
| | | State research skills needed by students in order to complete assigned research tasks. | | Criterion test to detect change in identified research skills in students. |
| | | Describe the way students perceive their assignments. | | Measure fidelity with which students perceive their assignments. |
| | | Suggest level of service needed at the media center in order to assist students with research assignments. | | Document evidence of change in reference services. |

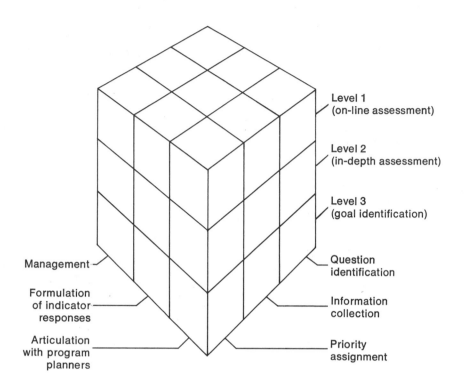

Level 1
(on-line assessment)

Level 2
(in-depth assessment)

Level 3
(goal identification)

Management

Question
identification

Formulation
of indicator
responses

Information
collection

Articulation
with program
planners

Priority
assignment

Note: Suggestions for identifying contributions of individual cells might include:

Purpose—     What is the unique contribution?
Population—   Who can best make this contribution?
Procedure—   How can the purpose be best accomplished?
Product—      What form should findings take to be congruent with purpose?

Fig. 6. CONSIDERATIONS FOR NEEDS ASSESSMENT
PROGRAM PLANNING

between the ideals of program planners and the realities of programs
(level 3). Discrepancies should also be expected to occur among the
priorities identified by the three levels. In many cases differences must be
reconciled because priorities are in conflict, whereas in other cases
priorities of one group will add to and amplify the work of another level.

After the coordinating committee managing needs assessment planning
determines that the concerns of the surveyed population are adequately
represented, then the process of assigning priorities begins. If the concerns are too numerous, some kind of grouping may be necessary before

considering priorities. One method for assigning priorities is to assemble persons representative of the total educational program, including the school media program, and to ask them to sort the concerns or needs in the form of questions which have been placed on cards. The question format tends to keep the discussion open and to avoid direct conflict until more information is gathered. Also, questions tend to imply the concerns rather than to ask for an early statement or goal that may reflect a dogmatic position (the media program budget is too large; the principal does what he wants with little regard for concerns of teachers and students). The sorting technique can include from three to five categories. If five categories are used, they may be labeled (1) urgent, (2) important, (3) moderately important, (4) unimportant, and (5) irrelevant.

Employing the card sort with homogeneous groups can be of value in several ways. For example, the assignment of priorities by administrators, media specialists, teachers, students, and community representatives can be a useful means of isolating conflicts to be reconciled among user groups. Card sorts made by representative groups and card sorts made by more or less homogeneous groups can be compared and given weight in a statistical sense. Dialogues should be encouraged; for example, administrators compare the way they have sorted their cards to the way students, parents, or teachers make their rankings. Dialogue can help each group to understand reasons for ranking and can produce a better balanced statement of needs.

Questionnaires can also be utilized to identify priorities. The questionnaire bypasses face-to-face interaction on the part of participants. The Delphi type process is superior to usual questionnaires because Delphi techniques involve several cycles whereby the respondent is able to consider the influences of information and the responses of other respondents. In other words, the Delphi yields a group consensus through the process of a controlled, indirect dialogue.

Those assembled to manage a needs assessment program (coordinating committee), the persons assembled to formulate the critical questions, and the population identified to provide information needed for responding represent three different groups. Each group suggests the different concerns and abilities that are appropriate. Individuals who ably articulate the critical problems may be a different group than those who are capable of suggesting indicator performance designed to detect degrees of problem resolution. For example, a teacher may complain that every time a student is sent to the media center for information the media specialist always replies to the student's request in the same manner: "Check the card catalog; if it's not there, we don't have it." Although this teacher has identified a need for better service, to suggest what changes are needed

propriate. On the other hand, the director of media services
ropriate indicator performance to be an 80 percent reduc-
... in this kind of response by the media specialist. The director may also
see a need to specify increased levels of reference service, including a
grater familiarity with the collection, as part of a professional in-service
program for the coming year.

A coordinating committee is knowledgeable about such theory and
practice of needs assessment techniques. In order to operate efficiently
as a decision making body, the committee should be composed of no
more than seven members if consensus is to be easily reached. Groups
identified for question formulation must represent every aspect and concern of the educational program. In many instances this group may be
synonymous with the total school population. In other words, all teachers
and students may be surveyed for a specific type of concern, or all parents in the community may be asked to respond in a given way. Information bearing on the questions identified will include both personal perceptions and a review of the literature.

The coordinating committee insures that the needs assessment (1) be
a continuously employed mechanism established as a part of the function of the management and administration of the school media program,
and (2) eventually produce stated ends congruent with objectives of the
educational program. The outcomes identified in any needs assessment
reflect the real world of the student, the teacher, media specialist, administrator, and community people as each relates to the educational program. In other words, the outcomes of a needs assessment must not be
theoretical, hypothetical, or philosophical but rather must be specific
concerns that are related to the desirable or undesirable outcomes of
programs.

### MEDIA PROGRAM

Weaving the functions of the media program into the fabric of the
curriculum demands a level and degree of planning not commonly found
in schools. A needs assessment is one example of planning that can help
integrate the media program with the school curriculum. Building an
educational media program that is completely integrated with the curriculum of a school makes it impossible to generate independently.

In the first place, the unique features of the school-community envi
ronment must be ascertained. The parameters for schools are set by
communities. What, in turn, the schools are allowed to do sets the standards for media programs. The political tenor of a local community, the
laws of the state and community, the physical restrictions of the school,

and even the geographical location of the school and the community within the state all impinge upon the kind of educational program that emerges. As the educational media program develops information resources in the community, the impact of power groups as well as the resources of professional organizations, state library agencies, and special libraries can all add dimensions or provide constraints to the program.

Any media program must relate to the environment in which it exists. Policy making should include key figures in management and curriculum development within the schools as well as personnel who can help extend the potential of the media program beyond the walls of the school. School library media programs that deeply penetrate their communities increase the potential of the programs and also clarify the purposes of the programs to the communities.

All media programs should have an effective mechanism for translating needs into objectives. The way the community is utilized depends upon the purposes and objectives of the educational media program and the curriculum of the school. A common yet erroneous concept relates to the sequencing of events in building the media program. For example, one might argue that only after the objectives of the media program are identified should the resources of the community be surveyed. In reality, they are parallel, each modifying the other and both existing together.

After objectives are set, alternatives must be identified for achieving them. Then, too, the demanded competencies and the necessary representation may form a different kind of organizational structure in order to identify and evaluate the alternative plans for goal realization. For example, a district may organize the office of the director of curriculum in order to create a structure for developing performance objectives from goal statements and translating objectives into tested instructional sequences as displayed in figures 7 and 8. The organization a school builds to translate goals into instructional sequences must be judged by its ability to carry out its mission of building an instructional program.

Criteria should be formed for all levels. What are the criteria for identifying the goals of the educational media program and for generating and selecting alternatives? By what criteria is the educational media program to be evaluated? The general rule for establishing the need for criteria relates to judgment. Whenever a judgment is necessary concerning a material, an operation, or the selection of personnel, the establishment of criteria is in order.

Developing criteria from the needs of students seems to be a reasonable place to start a library media program. However, there are at least three considerations. First, the needs of users as identified by psychologists and educators are at best hypothetical. Second, the needs of the

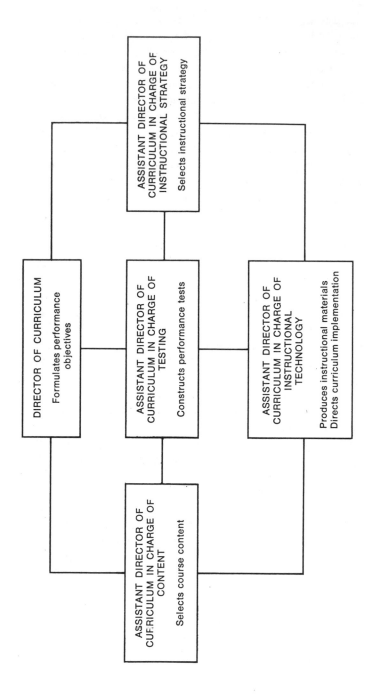

Fig. 7. FLOW CHART SHOWING SUBSYSTEMS IN THE DEPARTMENT OF CURRICULUM DEVELOPMENT

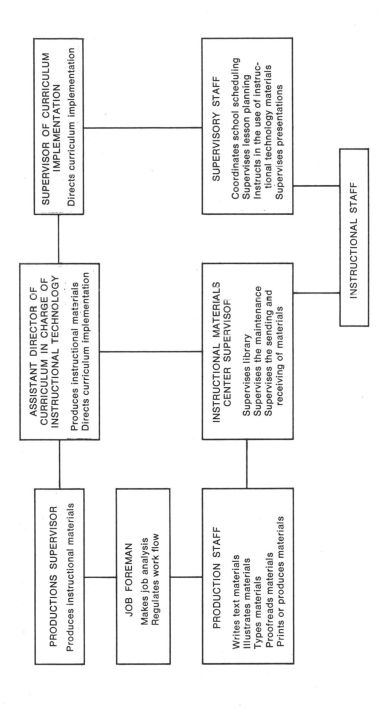

Fig. 8. FLOW CHART SHOWING THE ACTIVITIES DELEGATED TO THE ASSISTANT DIRECTOR OF CURRICULUM IN CHARGE OF INSTRUCTIONAL TECHNOLOGY

social order are more specific and are directly tied to the survival of the culture. Consequently, society makes demands and exercises control over education on all levels. Third, presently there is not an operational strategy for accurately determining user needs in advance.[14]

In many instances the differences between what is perceived to be good as far as an educational media program is concerned and what must be included in media programs cause many frustrations. In other words, media programs as well as educational programs talk about doing one thing while most of their energy is spent responding to other concerns and demands. The one hopeful solution is the establishment of functional criteria that are tied to the increased use of consensus in planning. Criteria represent a compromise among the forces that mold and control the media program. Both credibility and power to implement can be gained when criteria are established by carefully selected representatives. Program planning includes

1. defining and clarifying program outputs
2. identifying requisite operational and resource elements in cost
3. identifying needs and preferences for services by systematically involving clients in determining service priorities.[15]

Program identification and improvement must focus on the interfacing between components in an educational program. Components include people, materials, machines, facilities, purposes, processes, perceptions, and environments. Purposefulness is judged in terms of the degree schools are facilitating the development of self-actualized, acculturated individuals. Appropriateness of an experience must be viewed in terms of best educational practice and technological responsibility.

[14] James W. Liesener and Karen M. Levitan, *A Process for Planning School Media Programs: Defining Service Outputs, Determining Resource and Operational Requirements, and Estimating Program Costs* (College Park: School of Library and Information Services, Univ. of Maryland, 1972), p. 36.
[15] Ibid., p. 45.

**Implications for the Media Program**

1. Media program development and curriculum development are merging into one unit.

2. The media program and the educational program are the mesh of interfacings of students with other system components.

3. Management and administration, design, information, and consultation functions relate to specific operations of the media program and coordinate the media program with the curriculum of the school.

4. Typical operations include acquisition, production, reference, storage and retrieval, maintenance, distribution, evaluation, and research and development. A trend exists to combine operations under such titles as collections development and technical processing.

5. All functions and operations should be justified in terms of the interfaces they support.

6. Needs assessments are employed to identify what society expects of the educational program and what the educational program expects of the school and district media programs.

7. Needs assessments establish priorities from lists of expectations.

8. Three levels of needs assessment should be considered—on-line, in-depth, and goal identification.

9. Needs assessments yield real statements of desired program outcomes.

10. Knowing and being able to apply physical, mental, emotional, and social processes as they relate to such conditions as motivation, readiness, reinforcement, cueing, pacing, sequencing, and retention improve the interfacings students have with people, materials, and processes.

11. Media professionals of the future must apply both best educational practice and technological responsibility to the diagnosis and prescription of learning problems.

12. The reluctance of schools to move into functional patterns of differentiated staffing at least partially relates to (a) identifying the competencies that are needed and (b) locating personnel with the needed specific expertise.

**Problems and Activities for Research and Discussion**

1. Discuss the areas of competency you feel are needed in modern educational programs. Try to describe how each competency relates to the educational program as a whole.

**2.** Identify a desirable interface that should exist in a media program. For example, the student (user)

- ✓ has what he needs when he needs it,
- ✓ participates in forming and implementing media program policies,
- ✓ successfully uses appropriate indexes,
- ✓ designs and produces media to attain curricular objectives, or
- ✓ enjoys media.

After identifying an interface which you feel is particularly important, visualize the support system necessary to insure that the interface can take place. Write a paragraph explaining your visualization. Use the sample shown for ideas but not as a model. Try to be original.

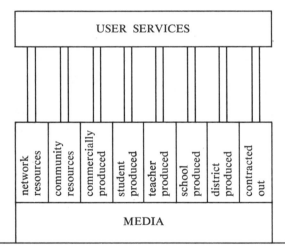

Diagram of a support system necessary to insure that the student has what he needs when he needs it.

*Sample Paragraph*

If students are to have the resources they need for individualized programs, all of the sources for providing material and people support must be identified and coordinated. Media that support the curriculum of the school and that are appropriate for varied learning strategies may be produced commercially by students and teachers, by media specialists, or by independent contracting. Community resources and networks may provide sources not available in the media center.

3. Using a chart similar to the one below, research and list ten indicators of best educational practice and of technological responsibility that relate to *all* of the functions of media programs—design, information, consultation, and management and administration. For example, employing cost-effective techniques to media programs not only relates to all of the functions but also is an indicator of technological responsibility. Establishing an integrated information system for a district is another example. Examples of best educational practice that are appropriate to all functions could include the development of genuine interpersonal relationships or the art of applying principles of motivation, pacing, or questioning strategies. The School Library Manpower's *Behavioral Requirements Analysis Checklist* (American Library Association, 1973) provides a rich source of ideas and interfacings that relate to both technological responsibility and best educational practice.

## GENERAL FUNCTIONS

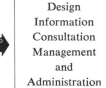

| Best educational practice requires information which increases the competencies of media professionals as they work with people. | Design<br>Information<br>Consultation<br>Management<br>and<br>Administration | Technological responsibility requires information which increases the competencies of media professionals as they apply scientific laws and principles to the design, implementation, and evaluation of the media program. |
|---|---|---|

*Indicators*                                         *Indicators*

1. ...........................          1. ...........................
2. ...........................          2. ...........................
3. ...........................          3. ...........................
4. ...........................          4. ...........................
5. ...........................          5. ...........................
6. ...........................          6. ...........................
7. ...........................          7. ...........................
8. ...........................          8. ...........................
9. ...........................          9. ...........................
10. ...........................         10. ...........................

Tracking Interfacings

PROBLEM. The educational or media program is different for each student because each individual interacts with people, materials, ideas, processes, and environments in his or her unique way. An educational program is improved when principles of best educational practice are applied. Best educational practice includes the positive application of what is known about motivation, readiness, reinforcement, pacing, sequencing, retention, and so on. Indicators of best educational practice may be observed as students interface with materials, ideas, processes, and environments.

ACTIVITY DESCRIPTION. Prepare a list of indicators of best educational practice for each item to be considered—motivation, readiness, reinforcement, pacing, sequencing, retention and so on. Have well in mind the practices that one may hope to find. Make arrangements to observe a student over at least a two-hour period in a variety of activities. The observation period may or may not be broken. Make sure that the student is not aware that you are observing his actions. Note that one interface may relate to best educational practice under several categories. In many instances recording of the data should occur after the observations. Brief notes taken during the observations should help with a more thorough analysis of the interfacings recorded.

OBJECTIVES. The student will (1) record the interfacings observed, (2) identify indicators of best educational practice, (3) suggest ways interfacings could be improved, and (4) share his findings with others.

EXAMPLE.

Description of the interface

*Teacher winks at student eagerly waving his hand to comment in response to the remarks being made by another student.*

Indicators of best educational practice

*The nonverbal behavior of the teacher may be reinforcing the student winked at ("I know you know.") and at the same time cueing the student talking ("John probably knows but let's see if you can't detect your own error.").*

What other principles could be employed?

*Other cueing techniques could be utilized. To help bring the problem into better focus, the teacher could question the student reciting. Being able to come up with the correct solution for oneself is a more rewarding experience than being told by the teacher or another student.*

## REFERENCES

American Association of School Librarians and Association for Educational Communications and Technology. *Media Programs: District and School.* Chicago: American Library Assn., 1975.

Bennis, Warren G. *Changing Organizations.* New York: McGraw-Hill, 1966.

Bennis, Warren G., and Slater, P. E. *The Temporary Society.* New York: Harper and Row, 1968.

Davies, Ivor K. *Competency Based Learning: Technology, Management, and Design.* New York: McGraw-Hill, 1973.

Gagné, Robert M. *The Conditions of Learning.* New York: Holt, Rinehart and Winston, 1970.

Gillespie, John T., and Spirt, Diana L. *Creating a School Media Program.* New York: Bowker, 1973.

Hamreus, Dale G., ed. *Media Guidelines: Development in Validation of Criteria for Evaluating Media Training.* Washington, D.C.: Bureau of Research, Office of Education, U.S. Dept. of Health, Education, and Welfare, June, 1970.

Herriott, Robert E., and Hodgkins, Benjamin J. *The Environment of Schooling: Formal Education as an Open Social System.* Englewood Cliffs, N.J.: Prentice Hall, 1973.

Hug, William E. "Promising Alternatives to Current Educational Practice." *Southeastern Librarian* 23:18-21 (Summer 1973).

Hussain, Khateeb M. *Development of Information Systems for Education.* Englewood Cliffs, N.J.: Prentice-Hall, 1973.

Jensen, Arthur R. "Understanding Readiness: An Occasional Paper." *Challenge* 1:6 (Nov./Dec. 1972).

Katz, William A. *Introduction to Reference Work. Volume 1: Basic Information Sources.* New York: McGraw-Hill, 1969.

Kaufman, Robert A. *Educational System Planning.* Englewood Cliffs, N.J.: Prentice-Hall, 1972.

Liesener, James W., and Levitan, Karen M. *A Process for Planning School Media Programs: Defining Service Outputs, Determining Resource and Operational Requirements, and Estimating Program Costs.* College Park: School of Library and Information Services, Univ. of Maryland, 1972.

Melcher, Daniel. *Melcher on Acquisition.* Chicago: American Library Assn., 1971.

Miller, Van, Madden, George R., and Kincheloe, James B. *The Public Administration of American School Systems.* New York: Macmillan, 1972.

School Library Manpower Project. *Behavioral Requirements Analysis Checklist.* Chicago: American Library Assn., 1973.

————. *School Library Personnel Task Analysis Survey.* Chicago: American Association of School Librarians, 1969.

Travers, Robert M. W. *Man's Information System: A Primer for Media Specialists and Educational Technologists.* Scranton: Chandler, 1970.

*Without a clear and detached examination of means and ends, purposes and ideals, the nation becomes a slave of its prejudices, the victim of its gadgets, and a casualty of its passions.*

IRWIN EDMAN

# Technology as Means

TEACHERS, MEDIA SPECIALISTS, and students need to become more adaptable as the techniques characteristic of future curriculum designs become part of the instructional program. Improving teaching and learning involves the structuring of environments which encourage the behaviors desired and discourage unproductive activities. The teacher in a single room with thirty-five students in a routine of tests, lectures, discipline, and once-a-week movies comprises an environment which inhibits certain students and teachers who have difficulty functioning under these conditions. Some teachers and students function happily with each student doing a different thing—in the media center, on the floor of the classroom or hall, on the lawn in the front of the school.

Installation of a new curriculum design encompasses more than simple in-service activities to teach personnel to function differently in the system. Researchers have pointed out frequently that the redesigning of instruction, materials, and schedules and the redeployment of personnel have failed to change the traditional relationships among students, teachers, processes, and media.[1] Educating people to function differently is more costly and less productive than accepting them as they are and changing their operational circumstances.[2] Once the needs of a curricu-

[1] Mary Elaine Wilsberg, "Effective and Ineffective Teacher Behavior as Viewed by Teachers in a Team Teaching Situation," *Dissertation Abstracts,* Vol. 26 (Nov. 1965), p. 2606.

[2] Amitai Etzioni, "Human Beings Are Not Very Easy to Change after All," *Saturday Review* 55:45-47 (June 3, 1972).

lum are established and facilitating environments provided, the interests and talents of the professional staff should be matched to the needs of the new system. It is impractical to reeducate for each new alternative.

ROLE OF THE MEDIA SPECIALIST IN THE TEACHING-LEARNING PROCESS

Responsibilities of media professionals as they relate to the selection, installation, and development of instructional systems will depend upon their levels of competence, special responsibilities, and the general structures within which they operate. Nevertheless, media professionals can reasonably expect to

1. evaluate and select commercially produced multimedia curriculum blocks for the school and district
2. participate in training sessions offered by the central district staff or commercial houses in the utilization and installation of specific educational products
3. train students and teachers to use mediated instructional units
4. participate in the teaching-learning team required for product development and implementation
5. modify both locally produced and commercially produced instructional packages.

Cost and extensiveness of some materials necessitate an elaborate evaluation and utilization plan. This is not to suggest that smaller instructional packages may not require attention for effective utilization. However, the cost factor involved in large systems of instruction makes it mandatory to evaluate carefully the materials. The expense may be less for purchasing and trying out small instructional units than assembling the expertise needed to thoroughly investigate before purchasing. Besides, even limited use of an inexpensive material may warrant its purchase.

The media specialist must look for unique features and valid processes when judging the potential of a commercially produced instructional package. A superficial preview of an instructional product frequently costing over a thousand dollars and providing for ten, twenty, thirty, or more hours of instruction cannot be tolerated. Many of these materials require specifically trained personnel. In large, extensive systems such as Westinghouse's Project PLAN, corporation consultants provide training for teachers to insure the effective installation of the system. However, instructional units provided by commercial houses rarely provide much more than a descriptive brochure designed to help teachers utilize the materials. The implications are that media professionals must start communicating in a different way with sales representatives and publication houses as well as with students and teachers in order to understand fully the procedures necessary for achieving maximum mileage from many educational products.

Today many school systems are encouraging teachers and students to work with media professionals to develop curricular materials, using the principles and practices of instructional design. On both the local school and district levels media professionals may be reasonably expected to

1. isolate student characteristics which may affect the instruction being designed
2. identify and construct performance objectives
3. construct criterion measures that assess the objectives identified
4. select content
5. plan activities in harmony with the learning requirements of each objective
6. participate in the teacher-learning program prescribed by the instructional module developed
7. evaluate and modify the instructional package.

Incorporating the process of instructional design into the educational program at the local school level demands a different approach than the incorporation of technological developmental processes at the district level in large, unified school systems. In the latter, professionals may be assembled to perform tasks with a high degree of sophistication. Teachers and media specialists working at the local school level can serve as part of the district team assembled to design instructional materials. They can provide insight into the nature of specific student populations and the characteristics of particular facilities. Local school personnel can field test and collect information for product developers. The expertise of district curriculum developers and professionals working directly with children can function as part of a research and development component of the total educational program.

A hypothetical situation will illustrate the possible role of the media specialist as he functions during the selection, installation, and development of educational materials. The director of curriculum requests the elementary school media specialists to participate with other professionals in the district in selecting approximately $3,000 worth of commercial multimedia packages for each of four areas—language arts, science, social studies, and mathematics. The director explains that four weeks during the summer are planned for this activity. The first week specialists from the language arts area will work with the group; the second week specialists from the science area will work with the group, and so on.

Media specialists from each of ten elementary schools, two elementary school principals, and the central office curriculum staff will work for the duration of the project. Further, the director states the intention to place a set of the instructional materials selected in each of the ten elementary schools in the district. The media center would be responsible for handling the logistics of the instructional packages. The total budget expenditure for multiple copies of these prepackaged, multimedia units is estimated to be $120,000.

The director of curriculum stresses that he hopes the best materials will be selected and that they will be compatible with the district's curriculum outline. He suggests three priorities. The first is to include materials that could replace current classroom work and allow students to work independently, on different levels, and at their own rates. In addition, the materials should provide the possibility of producing an increase in achievement over usual classroom experiences. The second priority is to include materials that could provide constructive alternatives for students who demonstrate difficulties in regularly scheduled and assigned classwork. The third priority is to include materials that could supplement or enrich the curriculum.

Sales representatives from publishing houses advertising self-contained, instructional blocks are invited to bring materials at appropriate times. The content, priorities, and levels are carefully described in a letter to each salesman.

The week before the selection process is to begin the director brings the subject matter specialists, media specialists, the two elementary school principals, and the staff of the department of curriculum development together, explains the summer's procedure, and asks for suggestions and questions. All agree that the subject specialists will

1. suggest the student population for which the materials are best suited
2. estimate where the material would best fit into the structure of the curriculum
3. ascertain the accuracy of the content.

The media specialists and principals are to investigate

1. what training is necessary for students and teachers for proper utilization of materials
2. how the training is best conducted
3. what time, personnel, equipment and space are needed for proper installation procedures.

The director's staff is to

1. evaluate field-testing data
2. examine the materials for their consistency in applying the principles and practices of good instructional design
3. analyze and make suggestions for methods of tracking, summarizing, analyzing, and reporting students' progress.

After discussing educational products with salesmen, after previewing materials, and after discussing considerations with other members of the various task forces, evaluations and recommendations supported by substantive statements will be presented by each group for each instructional resource under consideration. Because of the limited number of commercial materials that are expected to meet the criteria, it is believed that at the end of each week a consensus can be reached by the three groups of professionals.

At the closing of the orientation meeting, the director states that he hopes that the multimedia units selected will be successful and that students, teachers, and media specialists will be so familiar with their usage and design that he can start the following summer with a series of workshops for producing similar materials on a district basis. Teachers, media specialists, central office curriculum staff, principals, and selected students will participate in these production workshops. He continues by saying that after materials are found that better individualize the curriculum and that provide for more variety and versatility in the curriculum, then perhaps a series of such workshops can transform areas of the curriculum where commercial materials are not available. Besides, he concludes, good as it is to buy a curriculum already built, it is better to build one which is unique to the system.

Although this hypothetical case does not present a model which is to be considered an ideal situation for the selection of multimedia packages of instruction, it does provide functional descriptions of what people may be doing in a particular selection process. From this kind of a functional description the role of the media specialist in the teaching-learning process can be implied. For example, it is obvious that the director of curriculum is seeking materials that may be utilized by students in the media center in lieu of routine classwork. Chances are that the media specialist will be the one who has to generate enthusiasm in the student, help the student in time of trouble, and generally manage and monitor the learning. Although the media specialist most probably will not decide which students pursue which instructional blocks, he may be the one who must determine whether or not the student is progressing satisfactorily. The media specialist, in other words, may find himself in the position of recommending to a student's teacher that the materials are too difficult, too easy, or whatever. When criterion measures are part of the total instructional package, the media specialist may find himself in the best position, logistically speaking, to administer and possibly discuss the results of independent study with students.

In the hypothetical case, the media specialist's responsibility for providing in-service and consultative services in the utilization of the instructional blocks selected is suggested. Installation of multimedia, self-paced instruction often requires in-service preparation of teachers relating to the purposes, formats, and machine operations necessary to make the system functional. Neglecting to provide the proper instruction for use of complex materials may defeat a project before it begins. The training of student monitors or aides to function as part of the instructional program is also critical in many blocks of instruction.

Since the media specialist is constantly working with all kinds of educational materials, it is reasonable for the director to expect him to participate and make a substantial contribution in curriculum development workshops. The media specialist will be expected to contribute to the identification of student characteristics, objectives, content, activities, and evaluation procedures in the workshop to follow.

### SPECIFYING OBJECTIVES

Education always seems to be looking for a panacea, some one thing that will solve all educational problems. Team teaching, flexible scheduling, schools organized within a school, programmed instruction, and free elective systems are all attempts to improve the education in elementary and secondary schools. Imaginatively implemented, all have merit and can contribute to the solution of particular educational problems. On the other hand, overused and poorly implemented innovations have in many cases proved disastrous. One persistent problem is the rushing into new programs by school systems whose personnel do not have the capacity or potential for implementation. Another, more serious problem is created when school systems discard one program because it is unsatisfactory and replace it with a more complicated one. However, problems in a school system are more likely to be associated with the personnel involved than the educational scheme employed. The importance of personnel becomes evident when one considers the number of exemplary programs which deteriorate into mediocre programs simply because the leadership is lost.

This word of caution is given because of the spreading belief that behavioral, performance, or operational objectives are the answer to all of the educator's problems. Behavioral objectives are a beginning, not an end; they clarify what is to be done, not what has been done. The purpose of writing an objective is to guide the learner. Therefore, it must be lucid and explicit, not ambiguous, or unrealistic, or unattainable. Mager overstates the case for behavioral objectives and seems to ignore the difficult job of designing the teacher-learning system when he says, "If you give each learner a copy of your objectives, you may not have to do much else."[3] Subsequent books by Mager, however, seem to indicate that Mager himself is cognizant of the complexity of the problems. Behavioral objectives are only part of a total instructional system. There is not much sense in having the steering column without the car and vice versa.

Performance or behavioral objectives are only one part of a total teaching-learning system. Purposes for programs grow from the needs of people, individually and collectively. These purposes are translated into broad, general goals which in turn must be broken down into performance objectives. A performance, behavioral, or operational objective is stated in explicit terms that will indicate the kind of learning that students are expected to demonstrate. Instructors need operational objectives to make decisions about teaching-learning options and to determine if the learning identified has taken place. Clearly stated objectives are important when students help other students, when parents monitor homework, when teaching assistants work with students in the classroom or media center, and when students are simply explaining to others what they are doing and what they have learned. The goals of an educational program may bring into focus the area of concern, but it is the operational objective that describes in detail what specifically is to be done.

Many of the new programs demand that the objectives be stated in behavioral terms. To date no school has been able to assemble a complete set of behavioral objectives covering all activities. Although many argue that it is not advisable for all objectives to be behavioral, the majority of the new programs maintain that unless the achievement of students is assessed no real educational benefits can be claimed, nor can one adequately make an assessment unless objectives are behaviorally stated.

At first glance writing objectives seems to be a relatively simple process. Many can attest to the fact that at first they were sold on the value of performance objectives, but they later became bogged down and unable to get their intents on paper. One of the most common quagmires

    [3] Robert F. Mager, *Preparing Instructional Objectives* (Palo Alto, Calif.: Fearon, 1962), p. 53.

that prevents the teacher from producing functional objectives is the persistent use of terms that have personal value but have little meaning to students. For example, most teachers value critical thinking skills. The term *critical thinking skills* does not communicate to the student exactly what to do. Important areas such as this have to be broken down into such specific learning outcomes as (1) discriminates between facts, opinions, and inferences, (2) identifies errors in reasoning such as the non sequitur, (3) identifies substantiated and unsubstantiated generalizations, or (4) distinguishes between warranted and unwarranted cause and effect relationships.

The most universally recognized rules for writing behavioral objectives have been developed by Mager and are described as having three necessary components: name the act the student is to perform, define the conditions under which the act is to occur, state the acceptable degree of performance.[4] Naming the act that the student will perform means using verbs that have specific meaning; behavioral terms such as *labels, matches, paraphrases, rewrites, selects,* and *summarizes* are specific examples. Verbs that communicate an array of skills are not appropriate for behavioral objectives. Words such as *knows, understands, synthesizes, appreciates,* and *evaluates* fit into this category.

The conditions under which a specific act will be performed by a student set the parameters for the activity. The conditions are frequently called "givens." Given a newspaper, given a set of problems, given ten minutes, the student will do thus and so. The conditions under which the act will occur are important because they affect the teaching-learning situation. The conditions also serve as a kind of validity check for designing the educational experience. For example, if the objective is "Given a diagram of a microscope, the student will learn its use," the conditions are obviously inadequate for the student to learn to use a microscope. The criterion of acceptable performance can be expressed in many ways. If the student is given a microscope and told that he must learn to focus it, the criterion is obviously one hundred percent. On the other hand, if the student is to underline all of the verbs on a particular page, ninety percent accuracy may be acceptable. What constitutes acceptable performance is important to the students if they are to understand what they are expected to know and do. Following are some examples:

[4] Ibid.

| Conditions | Act | Criterion |
|---|---|---|
| Given ten sentences | *underline* each verb | with 90% accuracy. |
| Using a French-English dictionary and a French essay | *translate* the essay | with no more than ten grammatical errors. |
| Given three fraction problems | *solve* them | correctly in ten minutes. |

Forcing teachers and media specialists to prepare behavioral objectives when they show little aptitude for the task may not be worth the time, effort, and frustration involved. The attitude that seems to prevail is that if behavioral objectives are good then everyone should learn to write them. The tasks that are involved with the instructional design process may best be handled by people who show an aptitude for performing particular tasks. In other words, in writing behavioral objectives, in designing creative activities, and in assembling criterion measures, it is advisable to match the task to the aptitude rather than to attempt to train all media specialists to perform all functions equally well. Besides, it is probably more economical to match competencies with tasks than it is to wage a campaign to persuade everybody to participate in the total process. Parents, students, teachers, and administrators should understand why behavioral objectives are useful and how they function in an educational system, but they may not necessarily be asked to do the writing.

The continuum of purposes-to-goals-to-objectives suggests more than a simple broad-to-specific relationship. Curriculum planners, concerned with such things as scope and sequence, work with goals and general objectives. Those involved with the total picture need not become involved with the sequencing of a series of experiences designed to teach square root. Policy makers such as boards of education work with broad overarching educational purposes. Breaking statements of intent into categories that relate to specific populations can help establish the needed relationships between the various components involved in the instructional design process.

Critics of behavioral objectives frequently argue that all learning objectives cannot possibly take this mechanical form, that describing performance in this way stifles the creativity of a teacher, and that the time required for the preparation of behavioral objectives is unrealistic in terms of current teaching loads. Verbalizing some types of learning and designing criterion measures to test if the learning has taken place are probably out of the reach of some classroom teachers. Regardless of the difficulty of the task, any attempt to apply a reasonable, systematic method for communicating with more precision is an asset to both teachers and students. The teacher's ability to write operational objectives is considered one aspect of competency and is given considerable emphasis by many administrators.

Paradoxically, science teachers find writing behavioral objectives fairly easy and have a considerable number of models to use, while teachers in such areas as literature, drama, and fine arts have the most difficult job as well as the least amount of research to aid them in their task. All content is not equally adapted to the behavioral approach. Emphasizing the technical over the general aspects of an area of study runs the danger of emphasizing the unimportant over the important. For example, some would argue that appreciation in art is more important than how to mix a particular color. The advocates of behavioral objectives would argue that appreciation is a result of a combination of specific and frequently independent sets of behaviors, each of which can be put into behavioral terms.

Behavioral objectives frequently seem to ignore the function or potential of social interaction. Undoubtedly one of the most powerful elements in the process of education is social interaction. Many believe that the process of social interaction is more important than content. One certain thing is that regardless of the emphasis on content, social interaction takes place whether one wants to guide it or ignore it. Unfortunately, such statements as "I don't believe in behavioral objectives," "they are too mechanistic," or "they ignore the most important objectives of the school" too frequently are used to avoid the task of specifying what constitutes desirable social interaction and other difficult-to-describe behaviors. The fact that one has a poor set of behavioral objectives does not mean that objectives themselves are bad.

Others say that teachers simply cannot think in behavioral terms. This is perhaps true of some administrators, media personnel, and teachers, but not of the successful ones. Media specialists constantly think in behavioral terms as they face the problems of how to get Paul to sit down and use the material he requested, to help Mary to concentrate, to stop Harold from disturbing his neighbor, and to organize a requested book talk for Miss Jones' literature class. The aim is to communicate desired outcomes and provide the means for achieving them.

The writing of behavioral objectives may become an end in itself. Teachers and administrators can become so fascinated with the writing of behavioral objectives that they care to do little else. Such compulsion is, of course, a danger constantly present in the schools. Media specialists who spend most of their time absorbed in writing programmed instructional sequences may overemphasize this particular technique. Some biology teachers are so interested in drawing and labeling that they teach a better class in illustrating than in biology. One word is very important in education—proportion. Teachers and media specialists must seek proportion in all they attempt. Obviously, everything else cannot go unattended while a teacher or media specialist assembles hundreds of behavioral objectives for a problem in instructional design.

Other critics of behavioral objectives say that experts who limit their thinking to developing behavioral objectives in terms of content rather than dealing with the range of youngsters' classroom behaviors are reserving the easiest job for themselves. Some teachers express the belief that the forms of living behavior demonstrated by pupils take precedence and pervade the instructional and learning behaviors. Other teachers simply believe that behavioral objectives are not particularly useful.

At any rate, the psychological organization and mediation of content seem undervalued. That all behaviors expected in the classroom can be pinned down into a neat sentence or two is improbable. Consequently, teachers, media specialists, and administrators should not expect behavioral objectives to answer the needs of all problems. They are tools. Skillfully applied behavioral objectives are useful. Poorly conceived, they become frustrating and confusing to both teachers and students.

Opposition to Mager's objectives has been voiced by those who contend that educational goals should transcend simple cognitive or manipulative skills. The opposition speaks of "higher values" and "full understandings." The resolute behaviorist insists that general statements so frequently listed under the goals of a school can be broken down into a series of behavioral statements which have meaning to students. The behaviorists would further maintain that the goals often reflect a statement of purpose intended for the lay public rather than a statement meaningful to the instructional planner. For example, the teaching of good citizenship is a goal acceptable to the community. To be of any value in the designing of instruction, however, the component parts of good citizenship must be broken down and approached directly. The objectives that make up good citizenship must be stated in behavioral terms. What should students be doing who have this thing called good citizenship? The hard core opposition to behavioral objectives may be broken when the semantics are solved. All educators should want to educate. In order to do this, they must effectively communicate their intents to learners.

Well-conceived and properly written behavioral objectives clearly communicate what is expected of both students and teachers. To a large extent, communication is the name of the education game. Behavioral objectives hopefully communicate intent to a greater degree than more vague or general objectives. A frequent and valid criticism of education centers around the fact that in many instances the way to succeed is to figure out the teacher. Too much energy is spent trying to outguess the instructor. Examinations are too frequently a surprise. Examination questions are too often pulled together because they are easy to write rather than because they accurately test what has been taught. Students have a right to know precisely what is expected of them during a course. Instructional designers must be sure they have communicated their objectives carefully if they are to evaluate the teaching-learning effort. Besides, there is a kind of moral question involved. Should educators be free to function without stating their objectives so that they have specific meaning?

Large pieces of information and broad, complicated content masses need to be broken down into manageable, meaningful, small pieces. Many educators feel guilty because they are not doing what they somewhat vaguely feel they should be doing. Global, all encompassing goals are one source of such guilt. Global objectives are statements including several goals and objectives and are too abstract to be useful. Their authors confuse feasibility with aspiration. When objectives educators frequently espouse are carefully examined, the impossibility of attaining such high sounding goals with the resources available becomes apparent. To teach good citizenship and a cooperative spirit, to develop an attitude compatible with the good life, to develop an appreciation for fine literature, to fully understand the function of the human body are examples of objectives which leave the student with a vague idea and the teacher free to move in some general way toward the not-too-well-known. This type of general intent has led Mager to write, "if you're not sure where you're going, you're liable to end up someplace else—and not even know it."[5]

Establishing sequences is facilitated when the objectives for a unit are available. Global objectives do not lend themselves to sequencing. Anticipating the next step is difficult when objectives are unclear. To determine what a student has to know in order to attempt the objective is comparatively easy, and to determine the next step is also relatively easy if you know what has been mastered. For example, if an objective is to make a cut in a twelve-inch board with no more than one degree tolerance, a student must know what a saw is, what kind to use, and how to saw. Furthermore, the usefulness of being able to make a square cut can be demonstrated when combined with other skills into a project.

---

[5] Ibid., p. vii.

When instructional designers use behavioral objectives, ordering information into logical hierarchies is made easier as they learn which abilities lead to the mastery of others. The relative difficulty of things becomes more apparent. At present, there is little justification to sequencing. What a student has to know to continue and where mastery will lead must become evident if students are to be convinced of the importance of the educational endeavor.

The education of media specialists and teachers also becomes more meaningful when specifics can be planned for and evaluated. Behavioral objectives can help set up a model for analyzing and initiating behavior of both students and teachers. Stanford University's success in microteaching attests to the value of using behavioral objectives in order to initiate the neophyte teacher into the classroom. Small sequences are outlined, practiced, and attempted. These sequences are put together into larger and larger packages until the new teacher presents an entire class-long sequence. Micro-teaching is a scaled-down sample of teaching, just as a behavioral objective is a scaled-down sample of a global objective. To put it another way, micro-teaching aims to break down the complex act of teaching into simpler components so that teaching is possible and evaluation becomes more precise. It is impossible to try to replicate that which another has done unless it is spelled out in exact terms. Similar techniques hold promise for training media specialists to work with children in such situations as negotiating a reference question.

Behavioral objectives give positive direction to the selection of the content sample. Media specialists sometimes overlook the selection of the content sample, the materials needed by teachers to illustrate laws or principles. School media specialists should not attempt to locate everything known about a subject. Rather, they should be able to ascertain the users' specific problems and direct them to the necessary resources. The teacher who can state objectives behaviorally and who has a strong reserve of information can produce illustrations which have specificity, direction, and meaning. It is a poor policy to teach a specific and then try to rationalize why it was taught. It is a good policy to state the objective and then choose content which will specifically present the information needed.

In summary, educators disagree as to the value of behavioral objectives. The opponents say that behavioral objectives

1. seem to ignore the function or potential of social interaction
2. tend to undervalue the psychological organization of content
3. cannot be written in some content areas
4. become an end rather than a means to an end
5. assume that the product of an objective can be predicted.

The supporters of behavioral objectives argue that

1. properly written objectives clearly communicate what is expected of both students and teachers
2. large pieces of information and broad complicated content masses are broken down into manageable, meaningful, small pieces
3. establishing sequences is facilitated
4. ordering information into logical hierarchies is made easier
5. teacher training becomes more meaningful when specifics can be planned for and evaluated
6. behavioral objectives give positive direction to the selection of the content sample.

### CLASSIFYING OBJECTIVES

After global or general objectives have been broken down into a series of behavioral statements, these objectives must then be analyzed in order to investigate and choose among alternative designs for the teaching-learning system. The process of instructional design is not an entirely linear one. The classification of behavioral objectives may indicate that the instructional program growing from the stated objectives has been too narrowly defined. For example, an analysis of the objectives written may show that the instructional unit is concentrating on memorization. After this becomes evident, the designers may want to reflect upon the implications of the general objectives and attempt to write performance objectives that provide experiences on a variety of levels.

Categorizing objectives by components or descriptors that suggest the form of activity to be adopted helps designers to achieve both balance and cohesiveness. The three major areas into which objectives may fall are the cognitive area, the affective area, and the psychomotor area. The cognitive domain includes the categories of knowledge, comprehension, application, analysis, and synthesis.[6] The affective domain includes the categories of receiving, responding, organizing, and characterizing.[7] The psychomotor domain includes such areas as performing, manipulating, and constructing.[8] The classification of objectives into one of these categories may also be considered a somewhat artificial activity since a student rarely works exclusively in one domain. For example, in cognitive

---

[6] Benjamin S. Bloom, ed. *Taxonomy of Educational Objectives, Handbook I: Cognitive Domain* (New York: David McKay, 1956).

[7] David R. Krathwohl, ed. *Taxonomy of Educational Objectives, Handbook II: Affective Domain* (New York: David McKay, 1964).

[8] Jerrold E. Kemp, *Instructional Design* (Belmont, Calif.: Fearon, 1971), p. 21.

exercises the student is probably using some psychomotor skills and expressing an attitude toward the exercises. Nevertheless, identfying the primary thrust of an objective does help set the parameters and identify the priorities for designing a teaching-learning activity.

More simplistic descriptors have been suggested for analyzing objectives. One such plan categorizes objectives according to whether or not the primary thrust is verbal, whether or not the objective concentrates on the affective domain, whether or not the emphasis is to develop skills in discrimination, or whether or not the objective focuses on motor performance.[9] Still another system develops five categories of objectives which include identifying, naming, describing, ordering, and constructing.[10] Regardless of the descriptors utilized for the classification of objectives, the purpose for finding a system for categorizing objectives remains the same. In order to operate effectively and efficiently the system must derive teaching and learning strategies that are congruent with the objectives. The assumption is that the more congruent activities are with objectives, the higher the probability for success.

Classifying behavioral objectives as shown in table 2 involves the identification of the *primary thrust* of the objective so that the contribution of the objective to the student's total education may be recognized, understood, and appreciated. A category of objectives has a group of descriptors that explain the common elements of objectives so classified. For example, the first category of the cognitive domain—knowledge—groups objectives that relate to simple recall. Verbs such as *identifies, names, memorizes, defines,* and *lists* usually indicate the knowledge category. The rationale is that the ability to distinguish between, to recognize, and to name the category of the objective provides insight into the demands the objective will make on the system.

Even though the major thrust of an objective is cognitive, affective, or psychomotor, most objectives include some aspects of all three domains. In designing instruction, the affective and psychomotor dimensions of an objective which is classified in the cognitive domain may produce the facilitating environment that enables the learning to take place.

All categories of objectives are open ended in the sense that a category is never fully mastered. One can always know and comprehend more and find new applications for existing principles.

The categories of the cognitive and affective domains are arranged in hierarchical order. For example, knowledge represents the simplest of

[9] *Principles and Practice of Instructional Technology Workbook* (Palo Alto, Calif.: General Programmed Teaching, n.d.), p. 17.

[10] Vernon S. Gerlach and Donald P. Ely, *Teaching and Media: A Systematic Approach* (Englewood Cliffs, N.J.: Prentice-Hall, 1971), p. 80.

Table 2: COGNITIVE AND AFFECTIVE DESCRIPTORS

COGNITIVE DIMENSION

| COGNITIVE AREA | SAMPLE DESCRIPTORS | SOME INDICATOR VERBS |
|---|---|---|
| Knowledge | Behaviors include remembering names, facts, processes and procedures, concepts, and principles. | Names, memorizes, lists, selects, states. |
| Comprehension | Behaviors include understanding, translating, and interpreting messages (verbal, aural, symbolic, pictorial). | Defends, elaborates, illustrates, infers, paraphrases. |
| Application | Behaviors include utilizing principles and procedures to solve a variety of problems. | Applies, computes, constructs, demonstrates, solves. |
| Analysis | Behaviors include breaking down input into component parts and describing relationships between components that account for wholeness. | Identifies assumptions, fallacies in reasoning, relevancy, and originality. Selects, analyzes, discriminates. |
| Synthesis | Behaviors include creating something new by selecting, creating, and combining components. | Creates, composes, designs, integrates, reorganizes. |
| Evaluation | Behaviors include judging the value or worth by applying criteria and standards. | Judges, evaluates, appraises, assesses. |

AFFECTIVE DIMENSION

| AFFECTIVE AREA | SAMPLE DESCRIPTORS | SOME INDICATOR VERBS |
|---|---|---|
| Receiving | Behaviors include attending to sensory input (teacher, book, film). | Listens, accepts, attends, looks. |
| Responding | Behaviors include reacting and actively participating. | Answers, conforms, shows, chooses, volunteers, practices. |
| Valuing | Behaviors include valuing objects, people, and ideas. | Appreciates, believes, initiates, selects, prizes. |
| Organization | Behaviors include recognizing, combining, and resolving differences in values and beliefs. | Organizes, defends, rationalizes, synthesizes, generalizes. |
| Characterization | Behaviors include demonstrating a consistent and predictable personality, life style, and value system. | Practices, performs, demonstrates, maintains, verifies. |

behaviors, evaluation the most complex; receiving represents a low level of affective behavior whereas characterization is highly complex. Because of the nature of the categories of both domains, each category builds on the other. For example, composing a fugue for the piano immediately signifies the synthesis category: the composer has knowledge and comprehension of what fugues are, the ability to apply and to translate into a new form, and the ability to analyze the component parts of a fugue and the way they can be fitted together into a new musical composition. The same is true in the affective domain. The character of a person refers to his ability to put everything together, to form his life style, and to behave in a consistent, predictable manner. A person may be characterized by what he is willing to attend to, what he responds to, what he values, and the way he puts all this together as an individual.

Sequences are established when skills are logically grouped or when one activity depends upon the successful completion of another. Sequencing of educational objectives involves the structure of the content to be mastered. It is improbable that, given an instructional unit, all of the things that a student needs to memorize can be isolated and treated separately. There is a relationship between what a student knows and what he can do. Doing may require constant remembering of certain things. Rather than grouping objectives because they indicate certain levels or categories, sequencing must consider the dependent and independent relationships existing in the structure of a discipline.

The main criticism of classifying objectives centers around the semantical problems of finding agreement on descriptors and of the technical problems of systematically and consistently attaching labels for each objective. Unless the names and categories of objectives can be utilized for checking and proceeding in the total process of instructional design, the activity remains terminal and taxonomical by nature. On the other hand, objectives can be stated in terms of educational activities. If an instructional designer can work directly from the objectives, the classification of each objective may not be necessary. Besides, it may be argued that, if curriculum workers can accurately define their objectives, it makes no difference whether or not all categories are represented.

However, the better argument seems to be that the classification of objectives leads to the consistent use of a vocabulary which enables designers to talk accurately about problems of developing teaching-learning systems from objectives. In addition, classifying objectives brings to the attention of the designer the concentration and/or dispersion of skills required. If, for example, a unit requires only knowledge, the designer may want to consider some objectives and activities that develop translation and synthesis skills. On the other hand, if the objectives start with synthesis (typically reflected in an essay objective), the designer may see the necessity of developing knowledge and understanding of content before expecting the student to put the material together in an original work.

### DESIGNING TEACHING-LEARNING ACTIVITIES

Best educational practice includes practical experience and an understanding of research in such areas as motivation, readiness, retention, and transfer. In applying what is known about learning, best educational practice includes tasks like those identified by Gagné in *The Conditions of Learning*.[11] These include:

1. gaining and controlling attention
2. informing the learner of expected outcomes
3. stimulating recall of relevant prerequisite capabilities
4. presenting the stimuli inherent to the learning task
5. offering guidance for learning
6. providing feedback
7. appraising performance
8. making provisions for transfer ability of learning
9. insuring retention.

The actual teaching-learning process consists of these kinds of events, each performing a function in the total design.

Once the objectives are written and classified, the problem of designing teaching-learning experiences according to best educational practice and technological responsibility must be tackled. Even though the formal processes of instructional design are based on a rational and empirically derived set of procedures, the processes lack a dependable formula that insures matching activities to objectives. Consequently, the process of instructional design presently depends upon elaborate systems for testing activities to find out *what* happens. The concept of best educational practice must, therefore, take into account the experience of teachers. Also, what works in one situation may not work in another. In other words, instructional designers can apply procedures up to a point. Then they find that it is beneficial for them to consult with teachers about what they have found to be successful and to work directly with students.

---

[11] Robert M. Gagné, *The Conditions of Learning* (New York: Holt, Rinehart and Winston, 1970), pp. 302–43.

### ASSESSING ENTRY, EN ROUTE, AND TERMINAL BEHAVIOR

Assessment must faithfully reflect instructional objectives. Consequently, every item of every test a teacher prepares must relate to an instructional objective. If this rule is followed, most of the criteria that characterize quality tests have been achieved.

The primary concern of the teacher in evaluation is to assess behavior changes within a specific area of the total curriculum. The primary concern of the media specialist and other media professionals must be related to testing processes and procedures, especially as each relates to the media program and the development of instructional products.

Assessment is made on many levels. For example, assessment can be made of national, regional, state, and local objectives. Each level has an important function in the total educational process. Classroom teachers and media professionals should be aware of the national, regional, and state programs that contribute to their efforts.

Conflicts exist because teachers and media specialists, on the one hand, want to set up learning experiences which are fair, vital, and relevant while, on the other hand, testing programs are frequently developed that block learning goals. The disparity between what and how instructional designers want students to learn, and what and how students actually do learn expresses itself in at least six different ways:

1. Testing for the purpose of awarding grades may overemphasize competition and block the sharing of ideas.

2. Testing for the purpose of awarding grades stresses academic status at the expense of learning. As a result, good marks instead of performance become the goal.

3. Testing for the purpose of awarding grades frequently results in students spending too much time speculating about a test instead of concentrating on learning.

4. Testing for the purpose of awarding grades results in students frequently feeling that once the test has been taken and the grade awarded the content can safely be forgotten.

5. Testing programs frequently emphasize specific information instead of concentrating on the broad, unifying principles.

6. Tests too frequently emphasize the right or wrong, the black or white, failing to show the grey. The teacher and/or media specialist, therefore, becomes the keeper of answers rather than a facilitator of learning.[12]

[12] Herbert A. Thelen, "The Triumph of 'Achievement' over Inquiry in Education," *Elementary School Journal* 60:190-97 (Jan. 1960).

The idea of a criterion-referenced test as opposed to a norm-referenced test is relatively new. A criterion-referenced test is used to determine achievement according to an absolute standard in contrast to a norm-referenced test which is interpreted according to a relative standard. Consequently, the difference between these two kinds of tests is in the interpretation of the results. A norm-referenced test distributes scores. A criterion-referenced test determines what a student knows, what objectives have been mastered.

Norm-referenced tests are used to discriminate between high and low performance. Since there may be little relationship between what a student knows and where he places on a norm-referenced test, instructional designers should avoid the use of norm-referenced tests in order to determine how much each student knows about the subject sampled by the test. Grading "on the curve" is unwise because (1) the average ability of each group differs, (2) average ability changes from year to year, (3) grades may not indicate actual achievement, (4) grades may make unfair comparisons among students, (5) probability of a particular group forming a normal distribution is very low, and (6) chance for grading errors increases unless normal distribution is approached.

Curriculum development procedures utilizing the principles and practices of instructional design use criterion-referenced tests to (1) determine where students are in relation to where they and/or teachers want them to be and (2) evaluate the effectiveness of the teaching-learning unit.

The introduction to the learning task may indirectly indicate to students where they should be in order to attempt the learning unit. Although this is not the primary purpose of the introductory statement, these implications should not be overlooked. The following introduction might preface a sound filmstrip learning unit entitled "Behavioral Objectives: Strengths and Weaknesses":

> Few of us use language as precisely as we would like. To say exactly what we mean is more than a science; it is an art. Behavioral objectives should accurately state the student's task, minimum standards of performance, and the conditions of measurement. Even though this seems like a worthwhile endeavor, some disagree with the usefulness and appropriateness of behavioral objectives. This instructional unit summarizes arguments for and against the use of behavioral objectives.

Students may and possibly should assume that they must understand what a behavioral objective is, what minimum standards of performance are, and what constitutes conditions of measurement before they begin this unit. Simply reading the introduction is not enough to begin the work.

In order for a learner to succeed in any instructional sequence, he must enter the system with specific competencies. Individual teaching-learning sequences cannot take the responsibility for all necessary prerequisites.[13] Nevertheless, most sequences should honestly attempt to define and/or evaluate entry behavior in terms of needed prerequisites even though the introduction may imply the skills needed. Tests designed to estimate prerequisite skills (readiness, entry requirements) are called entry tests.

Entry behaviors may be relatively general or very specific. For example, if the purpose of a learning sequence is to present arguments for and against the use of behavioral objectives, the description of or measure for entry behavior may be relatively broad. Appropriate entry behavior for this unit may be the ability to discriminate between behavioral and nonbehavioral objectives. Remediation may be described in this case. In other words, the description of entry behavior may include a statement such as this:

> If you cannot distinguish between behavioral and nonbehavioral objectives, work Mager's program entitled *Preparing Instructional Objectives* before beginning the learning sequence.

On the other hand, prerequisite behaviors needed to understand the molecular activity in solids, liquids, and gases may be quite specific. The student needs to possess a concept of a molecule in order to develop an accurate understanding of how molecules behave together under specific conditions. Comprehension of the atomic theory may be developed in a preceding learning unit which the student may need to repeat. However, sophisticated designs should employ a variety of remediation strategies available to students enabling learning, reviewing, or relearning via a fresh new sequence.

Developing an operational system for identifying readiness is of prime importance to advanced curriculum designs. Learning can be individualized only to the extent that prior behavior can be determined and utilized in conjunction with an individual's learning style in order to prescribe the most appropriate learning design for the individual.

When students demonstrate readiness, they may enter the learning system. After studying the operational objectives for the learning sequence, students should know what they are expected to do after completing the sequence. Pretesting should also help students realize what they are expected to do after completing the unit. A pretest tells students

---

[13] James W. Popham and Eva I. Baker, *Planning an Instructional Sequence* (Englewood Cliffs, N.J.: Prentice-Hall, 1970), p. 54.

whether or not they need to complete the instructional unit, or what part they need to complete.

Pretesting should provide data to answer three questions: (1) Does the student already possess the terminal behaviors desired? (2) Does the student need only part of the instructional sequence? (3) Does the student need the entire instructional sequence?

En route behavior may be assessed at various points along the learning sequence. In programmed material the en route test is frequently called a "testing frame." This kind of en route testing checks to see if the student is ready to proceed or needs to repeat a sequence. Ideally, the student would be exposed to a new mode after failing to meet the criterion in one of the en route measures. Yet, it must be remembered that an en route test is in itself an instructional device which may be employed to summarize and bring into focus the preceding learning sequence.

En route assessment may take the form of observed performance, inventories, questionnaires, subjective tests, multiple choice questions, and so on. A simple pretest may be used for the learning unit entitled "Behavioral Objectives: Strengths and Weaknesses":

INSTRUCTIONS. Test your need for this learning sequence by completing the true-false test below.

_____ 1. Most behavioral objectives concentrate on social interaction.
_____ 2. Psychological organization of content is given too much emphasis by writers of behavioral objectives.
_____ 3. Some believe that behavioral objectives emphasize the technical at the expense of the more important aspects of a discipline.
_____ 4. All educational outcomes are predictable.
_____ 5. The opposition to behavioral objectives believes too much emphasis is given to "higher values" of the curriculum.
_____ 6. The weakest element of well-constructed behavioral objectives is an inability to break down large chunks of information.
_____ 7. Behavioral objectives make sequencing difficult.
_____ 8. Ordering information into logical hierarchies is made easier with behavioral objectives.
_____ 9. Behavioral objectives can help set up a model for analyzing and initiating behavior.
_____10. Behavioral objectives give positive direction to the selection of the content sample.

Simple assessment devices such as this true-false test should be well within the capability of the average designer. However, test makers should always strive for innovative ways to assess. Teachers and media specialists, like students, must start at a point they can manage before they advance to more sophisticated levels. Objective assessment devices are perhaps a good starting point. In addition, many behaviors must be assessed on the job, in the laboratory, or in other suitable environments as the student performs.

There is one overarching purpose for terminal evaluation: it helps the teacher determine the degree to which objectives have been achieved. As a result, evaluation should provide data which help answer the question: How effective is the teaching-learning sequence? Measures designed to assess terminal performance are called posttests.

Terminal assessment typically consists of observation, evaluation of exercises, and achievement testing. The difference between a "true" criterion measure and an achievement test is that a criterion measure tests for *all* objectives while an achievement test *samples* objectives. The difference between the pretest and the posttest indicates the amount of growth for each individual. Therefore, the two measuring techniques must be comparable. The easiest way to achieve this is to design like instruments. For example, if the broad objective of a learning unit is to improve the learner's ability to present a demonstration before a class, the obvious pretest and posttest involve observed performance. A multiple choice pretest and an essay item posttest are unlikely to do the job since they test different abilities.

Obviously, the specific learning task will require specific instructional objectives. Regardless of the variation that exists from task to task, learning outcomes usually fall into (1) knowledge, (2) specific skills, (3) general skills, and (4) attitudes, interests, and appreciations. Thus, the first step of the appraiser is to separate the objectives that are testable by paper-and-pencil tests.[14] Since these measuring instruments are the cheapest, the most easily produced, and frequently the most reliable (simply because more information is available), entry, en route, and terminal behavior should use paper-and-pencil tests whenever they will do the job.

At least seven characteristics of good appraisal instruments should be considered:

1. If possible, the validity of the techniques should be determined. The validity depends on the degree to which the technique measures what it attempts to measure.
2. Evaluation techniques must be reliable. Reliability is the extent to which a test is consistent, the extent to which it is dependable.
3. Evaluation techniques should adequately sample the desired behavior. If the testing technique is carefully constructed to evaluate the objectives, sampling should not be a problem. Sampling becomes a

[14] Norman E. Gronlund, *Constructing Achievement Tests* (Englewood Cliffs, N.J.: Prentice-Hall, 1968), p. 15.

problem when large numbers of mediated units are combined over an extended period.

4. Evaluation techniques should be objective. That is, personal judgments should not affect the scoring process or the results.

5. Evaluation techniques must be practical. The technique must be feasible to administer, be possible to finance, and be practical to score.

6. Evaluation techniques must be comparable to each other if they are to be combined. Comparability is not only important between and among entry assessment devices, en route measurement instruments, and terminal assessment measures but also between mediated instructiontal sequences which have been designed to function together.

7. Evaluation techniques must possess utility to the degree that they serve a specific need.[15]

### SEQUENCING, SELECTING, AND PRODUCING MEDIA

The complicated problem of handling the many variables that affect learning has retarded progress toward a comprehensive theory of instructional design. Many have attempted to design materials to be "teacher proof" in order to eliminate the many variables that are also associated with the instructor. Selection of media and their placement in learning experiences cannot be effective without a way of relating materials to the learning process. Despite the influence of age, experience, motivational level, and general health, there are considerations which will improve the establishment of sequences, selection of materials, and production of materials that assist a student in achieving objectives.

The justification for sequences has been traditionally associated with the developmental structure of a discipline. For example, history is frequently divided into chronological segments, the study of biology commonly begins with the cell and ends with the study of the organism in its environment, and so on. The reasons for arranging topics in sequence is usually logical in terms of content but may or may not consider the dependent-independent relationships that exist between topics or the developmental level of the student. The decision to study the geography of South America before the geography of Africa is probably more arbitrary than rational. On the other hand, learning how to multiply is prerequisite to learning long division. Identifying what a student needs to master before he takes the next step is an important consideration for

---

[15] J. Raymond Gerberick, H. A. Green, and A. N. Jorgensen, *Measurement and Evaluation in the Modern School* (New York: David McKay, 1962), pp. 52–68.

the instructional designer. Likewise, identifying those competencies that can be learned at many developmental levels and in many orders can make various segments of the curriculum more versatile and less artificial. Artificial sequences lack justification in terms of content and the developmental level of the learner. If schools can identify the steps necessary in some disciplines and break the curriculum up in areas that are frozen into unnatural sequences, the places where flexibility is feasible or where tight programming is necessary become clearer.

Sequencing, selecting, and producing media that meet the specific demands of curriculum objectives depend upon the degree that readiness can be ascertained. The concept of readiness includes identification of prerequisites that precede the learning event. Gagné defines readiness as "a developmental state at which a child has the capacity to receive instruction at a given level of difficulty or to engage in a particular activity."[16] Relationships between internal and external conditions necessary for the learning event must be determined. In this regard the use of many kinds of materials in many formats and the application of varied classroom techniques provide a greater range of stimuli for the learner. This increases the mathematical probability that previous experience will be tapped.

Individual growth rates and experiential backgrounds are of primary importance when planning an individualized curriculum. The learning event provides a stimulus situation, whereas the resulting action forms the response. The major role that stimulus and response play in learning is a key factor in readiness.

> There is a very fundamental point that each learner approaches each new learning task with a different collection of previously learned prerequisite skills. To be effective, therefore, a learning program for each child must take fully into account what he knows how to do already. One must find out what prerequisites he has already mastered—not in a general sense, but in a very precise sense for each learner.
> Instruction becomes not primarily a matter of communicating something that is to be stored. Instead, it is a matter of stimulating the use of capabilities the learner already has at his disposal, and of making sure he has the requisite abilities for the present learning task, as well as for many more to come.[17]

The identification of stimulus and response pairs can help bypass the tendency to organize instruction around content outlines. Thinking in terms of stimulus and response stresses what a learner needs to be able

---

[16] Gagné, *Conditions of Learning*, p. 3.
[17] Robert M. Gagné, "Some New Views of Learning and Instruction," *Phi Delta Kappan* 51:471 (May 1970).

to do before beginning an instructional sequence as well as what he is able to do during a teaching-learning sequence. The basic concept of stimulus response pairs relates to sequencing by identifying subtasks for any given objective. An empirically derived system which helps learners to identify the steps necessary to achieve a specific objective will not only help the learner achieve his objectives but also identify more accurately the space, time, and instructional resources necessary for a particular teaching-learning unit. Precision in identification of interim steps helps solve the mystery of how a particular competency is gained. This, in turn, provides much better information for the identification of possible alternatives for sequence improvement.

In order to clarify how stimulus response pairs may apply in the sequencing, selecting, and producing of educational media, a sample case is presented. An objective of a biology class is: Given a leaf, microscope, and water mounting equipment, the student will locate and diagram the stomata of a leaf. In order to design or select a teaching-learning sequence that will provide the necessary experience, the teacher should analyze each step to be included in the learning sequence. Table 3 lists tasks (subobjectives, enabling objectives, or interim objectives) and shows stimulus response pairs for a particular objective.

When objectives are broken in this fashion, sequencing becomes clear and criteria for selecting or producing a teaching-learning unit can easily be developed. When tasks are spelled out at this level, the readiness of students may also be ascertained. For example, if students are familiar with making water drop mounts, the tasks that relate to this procedure may be eliminated. On the other hand, if students have not used a microscope before, then the objectives which relate to placing a slide under the microscope and locating the stomata would have to be broken down into all of the steps that are necessary for students to operate the microscope.

The way that subobjectives are most frequently identified involves the close observation of a task as it is being performed. In other words, if persons designing this sequence did not know how to prepare the epidermis of the underside of a leaf in order to show the stomata, they would have to observe someone who is proficient in this task in order to determine the stimulus and response pairs as they are naturally sequenced.

The evaluation of what students know or can do after viewing a film, listening to a tape, or proceeding through a multimedia package presents a complex problem. Obviously, the identification of what happens when a student interacts with media has far-reaching implications for sequencing, selecting, and producing media. The theory is that after tasks indicated by a specific behavioral objective are identified and sequenced, a

Table 3: TASKS AND STIMULUS RESPONSE PAIRS

Objective: Given a leaf, microscope, and water mounting equipment, the student will locate and diagram the stomata of a leaf.

| TASK (subobjective, enabling objective, or interim objective) | STIMULUS | RESPONSE |
|---|---|---|
| 1. Given a leaf, locate the underside. | leaf | place leaf underside up |
| 2. Hold leaf between thumb and forefingers of each hand so that the thumbs are touching. | leaf | hold leaf |
| 3. Moving the right hand away from your body and the left hand toward your body, tear the leaf so that the thin "skin" on the underside separates. Repeat if necessary. | leaf | tear |
| 4. Place a drop of water on the middle of the slide. | water and slide | put drop on slide |
| 5. Float a tiny piece of the transparent "skin" on the water drop. | "skin", water, and slide | float "skin" |
| 6. Place a cover slip gently over the water drop. | slide and cover slip | put cover slip on water drop |
| 7. Place the prepared slide under microscope and locate stomata. | slide and microscope | locate and focus |
| 8. Diagram several stomata. | paper and pencil | draw diagram |

better system for selecting and producing media can be developed.

Tosti and Ball refer to the learning event as the presentation form. The presentation form results from a combination of five considerations:

1. What encoding forms such as realia (environment), pictures, symbols, or verbal descriptions can provide the needed stimulus? What are the limitations to each form identified? How can the limitations be overcome?

2. What kinds of interaction seem to be indicated? When is it logical to request a student to listen, read, write, choose, draw, recite, jump, run, select, and so forth? What are the limitations to the kind of interaction identified? How can the limitations be overcome?

3. What considerations affect the management of the presentation? Must the management take into consideration the long-range plans of a student, the attainment of a specific objective, the provision of activities designed for enrichment, and/or the structuring of moti-

vational environments? What are the limitations of each management system identified? How can the limitations be overcome?

4. What time is necessary for the task and what are the implications of the time dimension as they relate to media? Is the media time-locked like a film? Does the task seem to call for a more individualized, persistent form such as a diagram? What are the limitations to the experience each provides? How can the limitations be overcome?

5. How can the presentation be sequenced (distributed) for maximum effectiveness? How does the sequencing of the presentation provide for drill, review, motivation, and so forth? What are the limitations of selected sequences? How can the limitations be overcome?[18]

Another procedure for choosing educational media has been developed by Briggs, Gagné, and May. Steps necessary for selecting media are:

1. formulate objectives
2. identify type of learning
3. design program utilizing required conditions of learning
4. prepare instructional options
5. make trade-off analysis and
6. write instructional specifications.[19]

Simplistic methods for sequencing, selecting, and producing media are being replaced by more scientific, although highly complex and time consuming, procedures (for example, stimulus-response pairs, chaining). Selecting materials through evaluative checklists that consider such things as publication date, reputation of author, accuracy of information, format, style and so forth is being criticized by those who say that the only important thing to consider in the selection of a piece of media is what a student knows or can do after interaction. The critics of traditional methods of selection are concerned with media as ways to learn which can be more directly tied to the total school curriculum. Producing media that relate to some general topic is being deemphasized as more and more materials are produced that develop specific, stated objectives. Only time will tell whether these new techniques will replace,

---

[18] Donald T. Tosti and John R. Ball, *A Behavioral Approach to Instructional Design and Media Selection* (Albuquerque: Behavior Systems Division, Westinghouse Learning Corp., 1969), pp. 23-52.

[19] Leslie J. Briggs *et al., Instructional Media: A Procedure for the Design of Multi-Media Instruction, A Critical Review of Research, and Suggestions for Future Research* (Pittsburgh: American Institutes for Research, 1967), pp. 28-29.

modify, or simply complement traditional procedures. Regardless of the strengths or weaknesses of the new procedures, there is no doubt that traditional procedures for sequencing, selecting, and producing media need to be improved. Accommodating hopeful new strategies seems to constitute a positive step forward.

## Implications for the Media Program

1. As the potential of media is extended, so are the functions of the media center and the media specialist. As educational media become more specific and precise, the media specialist becomes an integral part of the educational program. In this context, media, media specialists, and other professionals will provide experiences which will supplement, transform, and replace activities traditionally found in the classroom.

2. Selecting, constructing, and installing of educational media provide entry points for the media specialist in the process of curriculum genesis, implementation, and renewal.

3. As media centers become more and more complex, attention must be given to identifying tasks and matching personnel with functions to be performed.

4. The media center must become a laboratory for in-service activities and workshops in curriculum development. As an expert in materials and instructional design procedures, the media specialist will serve as a consultant in the teaching-learning process.

5. The media center will increasingly assume the responsibility of monitoring, managing, and evaluating students as they work on self-instructional modules and produce media which expand a student's communication skills.

6. The media center may grow to include a depository for banks of behavioral objectives, instructional packages produced by students and teachers, and evaluation devices constructed for specific purposes.

7. The media specialist must be just as comfortable discussing classification schemes designed to organize areas of cognition, learning conditions, or encoding forms as he has been discussing fiction, nonfiction, films, filmstrips, magazines, or reference works. The media center and the media specialist must be able to provide information on current processes and innovative strategies in terms of strengths and weaknesses and in terms of constructive alternatives.

8. Whether dealing with a reference question or a problem in instructional design, the media specialist must be able to diagnose the need in terms of the kind of learning involved and must attempt to provide mate-

rials that will more specifically relate to the user's need. Diagnosing the learning requirements of a performance objective is not basically different from negotiating a reference question except for the fact that the latter has not incorporated the know-how of the former.

9. Media centers must continue to rely on concepts of best practice and experience and incorporate empirically-based processes into the operation of media centers.

10. Media are increasingly utilizing accountability (assessment) systems which are a part of the total design of the product. As a matter of fact, the objectives and criterion measures in a mediated learning unit provide the constraints for the activities developed in the package. Failure to see the relationships is a failure to understand both the format and the content.

11. Sequencing, selecting, and producing media depend on a concept of readiness. Readiness is the key to appraising appropriateness, to selecting the right material for the right user, and to deciding what to include in a particular instructional sequence.

---

## Problems and Activities for Research and Discussion

1. Isolate and discuss factors which must be considered when introducing a new educational product into the curriculum.

2. Review five teaching-learning packages. Describe (a) the appropriate target population, (b) the presence, absence, and/or appropriateness of criterion measures, (c) the presence, absence, and/or appropriateness of objectives as they relate to evaluation procedures, and (d) the appropriateness of the content and activities provided in respect to criterion measures and/or objectives.

3. Choose a learning material such as a film or filmstrip and list the concepts and skills a student needs in order to comprehend and utilize the content presented (entry behavior, prerequisites, readiness).

4. List and develop three functional and three political obstacles associated with the emerging role of the media specialist in the teaching-learning process.

5. Label each of these statements as follows: G = General Goal, C = Cognitive Objective, A = Affective Objective.

    _____ (a) The educational media program must continually assess the needs of users and evaluate the alternatives for providing for these needs.

    _____ (b) Students will voluntarily increase their use of the media center.

——— (c) Given a topic, the student will locate six articles relating to the topic by using the *Readers' Guide to Periodical Literature.*

——— (d) The media center will increase its involvement with in-service activities for teachers.

——— (e) Students coming to the media center are greeted by a sincere, "glad you have come" smile.

——— (f) Given a list of materials, the student will be able to select the materials which should be placed in the vertical file.

6. Select the most probable cognitive area for each of the following statements.

> k  knowledge
> c  comprehension
> ap  application
> an  analysis
> s  synthesis
> e  evaluation

——— (a) The student will list in order all of the kings and queens of England with only two errors in spelling permitted.

——— (b) The student will translate a paragraph describing fluctuations in populations of the United States into a bar graph.

——— (c) Formulate and apply criteria for judging the value of an educational media program.

——— (d) Given a political speech, identify at least five errors in logic.

——— (e) Given a defend-or-refute topic, develop an essay from a selected point of view.

7. Explain how the categories of the cognitive and affective domains are arranged in hierarchial order.

8. Discuss the difference between a criterion-referenced and a norm-referenced test.

9. Defend the statement: Readiness is the key to understanding user needs.

---

**Sample Minimodule**

Making a Module

PROBLEM. Talking about designing instruction is easier than the task. Nevertheless, competency in instructional design can provide an entry point for the media specialist in the curriculum development process.

Although the text materials are not intended to be used by those studying to be instructional designers, the chapter does provide enough information for a "first try" at building a simple module. Select a small topic like one of the following: locate a book in the card catalog; set up a specific kind of filmstrip projector; use a specific reference book; use the Cutter table; prepare an order card; use accession numbers.

PERFORMANCE OBJECTIVE. Using the process and suggestions provided, construct a minimodule. Following are enabling objectives with suggestions for development.

1. State and discuss the general problem or point of concern. Develop the need to know or be able to do what is developed in the module. Be brief and try to be as interesting as possible. A quotation, story, metaphor, or simile may be employed which could bring the problem into focus. Page vii of Mager's book entitled *Preparing Instructional Objectives* is an excellent example of an attention-getting device.

2. Formulate performance objective(s). Break down the general problem or goal into statements describing exactly what the learner is expected to do. The objective should state the conditions, the terminal performance desired, and the standard. If this is all a bit fuzzy, read Mager's book entitled *Preparing Instructional Objectives*. After it is clear what a performance objective is, the following suggestions may help in generating the objectives needed.

    a. If you cannot produce the objective, try to write a test item for the thing you feel ought to be learned.

    b. If you have a good idea for an activity which you believe will develop the competency desired, develop the activity, analyze it, and try to "visualize" what a student may learn from completing the activity. Put these down in simple statements along with how you will know if the student has learned what you feel he ought to.

    c. Ask a student to try out the activity. Ask him what he thinks he has learned from it. Tell him what you hoped it would accomplish.

    d. Look at the objectives that others have developed.

3. State entry requirements (readiness, prerequisites). Spell out any competencies a student needs before beginning the minimodule. For example, basic skills in cataloging, materials production, reference, and so forth, may be necessary for the successful entry of a student.

4. Construct a pretest. This should tell prospective students whether or not the teaching-learning unit is needed.

5. Design the teaching-learning event. Give complete instructions and bibliographic information for any materials students are to use. Generate the program or learning sequence so that the minimodule is self-contained. Use a combination of activities and materials. Select a strategy that fits the task at hand.
6. Construct the criterion measures. Assess each objective.
7. Try out the minimodule on a friend. Discuss the potential of this type of instruction. How many of the ideas presented in the chapter have been included? How could the minimodule be improved?

CRITERION MEASURE. The finished module must contain a workable model of the seven sections outlined.

### REFERENCES

Ahmann, J. Stanley, and Glock, M. D. *Evaluating Pupil Growth*. Boston: Allyn and Bacon, 1958.

Bloom, Benjamin S., ed. *Taxonomy of Educational Objectives, Handbook I: Cognitive Domain*. New York: David McKay, 1956.

Briggs, Leslie J. *et al. Instructional Media: A Procedure for the Design of Multi-Media Instruction, A Critical Review of Research, and Suggestions for Future Research*. Pittsburgh: American Institutes for Research, 1967.

Bruner, Jerome S. *Toward a Theory of Instruction*. Cambridge: Harvard Univ. Pr., 1966.

Canfield, Albert A. "A Rationale for Performance Objectives." *Audiovisual Instruction* 13:127-29 (Feb. 1968).

Etzioni, Amitai. "Human Beings Are Not Very Easy to Change after All." *Saturday Review* 55:45-47 (June 3, 1972).

Gagné, Robert M. *The Conditions of Learning*. New York: Holt, Rinehart and Winston, 1970.

————. "Some New Views of Learning and Instruction." *Phi Delta Kappan* 51:471 (May 1970).

Gerberick, J. Raymond, Green, H. A., and Jorgensen, A. N. *Measurement and Evaluation in the Modern School*. New York: David McKay, 1962.

Gerlach, Vernon S., and Ely, Donald P. *Teaching and Media: A Systematic Approach*. Englewood Cliffs, N.J.: Prentice-Hall, 1971.

Gronlund, Norman E. *Constructing Achievement Tests*. Englewood Cliffs, N.J.: Prentice-Hall, 1968.

Haberman, Martin. "Behavioral Objectives: Bandwagon or Breakthrough." *Journal of Teacher Education* 19:91-94 (Spring 1968).

Kemp, Jerrold E. *Instructional Design*. Belmont, Calif.: Fearon, 1971.

Krathwohl, David R., ed. *Taxonomy of Educational Objectives, Handbook II: Affective Domain*. New York: David McKay, 1964.

Mager, Robert F. *Goal Analysis*. Belmont, Calif.: Fearon, 1972.

————. *Preparing Instructional Objectives*. Palo Alto, Calif.: Fearon, 1962.

Mager, Robert F., and Pipe, Peter. *Analyzing Performance Problems or 'You Really Oughta Wanna.'* Belmont, Calif.: Fearon, 1970.

The National Special Media Institutes (NSMI). *The Affective Domain.* Washington, D.C.: Gryphon House, 1972.

———. *The Cognitive Domain.* Washington, D.C.: Gryphon House, 1972.

———. *The Psychomotor Domain.* Washington, D.C.: Gryphon House, 1972.

Popham, James W., and Baker, Eva I. *Planning an Instructional Sequence.* Englewood Cliffs, N.J.: Prentice-Hall, 1970.

*Principles and Practice of Instructional Technology Workbook.* Palo Alto, Calif.: General Programmed Teaching, n.d.

Thelen, Herbert A. "The Triumph of 'Achievement' over Inquiry in Education." *Elementary School Journal* 60:190-97 (Jan. 1960).

Tosti, Donald T., and Ball, John R. *A Behavioral Approach to Instructional Design and Media Selection.* Albuquerque: The Behavior Systems Division, Westinghouse Learning Corp., 1969.

Ullmer, Eldon J., and Stakenas, Robert G. *Instructional Development Handbook.* Tallahassee: Florida State Univ., Division of Instructional Research and Service, 1971.

Wilsberg, Mary Elaine. "Effective and Ineffective Teacher Behavior as Viewed by Teachers in a Team Teaching Situation." *Dissertation Abstracts* 26:2606 (Nov. 1965).

# Bibliography

Ahmann, J. Stanley, and Glock, M. D. *Evaluating Pupil Growth*. Boston: Allyn and Bacon, 1958.

Aiken, Henry D. *The Age of Ideology*. New York: Macmillan, 1932.

American Association of School Librarians and Association for Educational Communications and Technology. *Media Programs: District and School*. Chicago: American Library Assn., 1975.

Anderson, Vernon E. *Principles and Procedures of Curriculum Improvement*. 2nd ed. New York: Ronald Pr., 1965.

Association for Supervision and Curriculum Development. *Perceiving, Behaving, Becoming*. Washington, D.C.: The Association, 1962.

Banathy, Bela H. *Instructional Systems*. Belmont, Calif.: Fearon, 1968.

Bayles, Ernest E. *Democratic Educational Theory*. New York: Harper, 1960.

Beadle, Muriel. *A Child's Mind*. Garden City, N.Y.: Doubleday, 1970.

Belson, William A. *The Impact of Television*. Hamden, Conn.: Archon, 1967.

Bennis, Warren G. *Changing Organizations*. New York: McGraw-Hill, 1966.

Bennis, Warren G., and Slater, P. E. *The Temporary Society*. New York: Harper and Row, 1968.

Berlo, David K. *The Process of Communication*. New York: Holt, Rinehart and Winston, 1960.

Bertalanffy, Ludwig von. *General System Theory*. New York: George Braziller, 1968.

Bloom, Benjamin S., ed. *Taxonomy of Educational Objectives, Handbook I: Cognitive Domain*. New York: David McKay, 1956.

Boles, Harold W. *Step by Step to Better School Facilities*. New York: Holt, Rinehart and Winston, 1965.

Borg, Walter R. *Educational Research: An Introduction*. New York: David McKay, 1963.

Breed, Frederick S. *Education and the New Realism*. New York: Macmillan, 1939.

Bretz, Rudy. *A Taxonomy of Communication Media*. Englewood Cliffs, N.J.: Educational Technology Publications, 1971.

Briggs, Leslie J. et al. *Instructional Media: A Procedure for the Design of Multi-Media Instruction, A Critical Review of Research, and Suggestions for Future Research*. Pittsburgh. American Institutes for Research, 1967.

Brix, V. H. *You Are a Computer*. New York: Emerson, 1970.

Broudy, Harry S. *The Real World of the Public Schools*. New York: Harcourt Brace Jovanovich, 1972.

144

Broudy, Harry S., Smith, B. Othanel, and Burnett, Joe R. *Democracy and Excellence in Secondary Education*. Chicago: Rand McNally, 1964.

Brubacher, John S., ed. *Modern Philosophies and Education*. Chicago: National Society for the Study of Education, 1955.

Bruner, Jerome S. *Toward a Theory of Instruction*. Cambridge: Harvard Univ. Pr., 1966.

Canfield, Albert A. "A Rationale for Performance Objectives." *Audiovisual Instruction* 13:127-29 (Feb. 1968).

Center for the Study of Evaluation. *A Guidebook for CSE Elementary School Evaluation Kit*. Boston: Allyn and Bacon, 1972.

Churchman, C. West. *The Design of Inquiring Systems*. New York: Basic Books, 1971.

Community National Field Task Force on the Improvement and Reform of American Education. *A Real Alternative: The Final Report and Recommendations of the Community National Field Task Force on the Improvement and Reform of American Education*. Publication No. OE-74-12007. Washington, D.C.: Dept. of Health, Education, and Welfare, 1974.

Cordasco, Francesco. *A Brief History of Education*. Paterson, N.J.: Littlefield, Adams, 1963.

Craig, Robert L., and Bittel, Lester R., eds. *Training and Development Handbook*. New York: McGraw-Hill, 1967.

Cyrs, Thomas E. Jr., and Lowenthal, Rita. "A Model for Curriculum Design Using a Systems Approach." *Audiovisual Instruction* 15:16–18 (Jan. 1970).

Daniels, Alan, and Yeates, Donald, eds. *System Analysis*. Palo Alto, Calif.: Science Research Associates, 1971.

Davies, Ivor K. *Competency Based Learning: Technology, Management, and Design*. New York: McGraw-Hill, 1973.

Davies, Ruth Ann. *The School Library: A Force for Educational Excellence*. 2nd ed. New York: Bowker, 1974.

Dougherty, Richard M., and Heinritz, Fred. J. *Scientific Management of Library Operations*. New York: Scarecrow, 1966.

Elam, Stanley. *Performance-Based Teacher Education*. Washington, D.C.: American Association of Colleges for Teacher Education, 1972.

————, ed. *Education and the Structure of Knowledge*. Chicago: Rand McNally, 1964.

Erickson, Carlton W. H. *Administering Instructional Media Programs*. New York: Macmillan, 1968.

Etzioni, Amitai. "Human Beings Are Not Very Easy to Change After All." *Saturday Review* 55:45-47 (June 3, 1972).

Foshay, Arthur W. *Curriculum for the 70's: An Agenda for Invention*. Washington, D.C.: National Education Association, Center for Study of Instruction, 1970.

Frederick, O. I., and Farquear, L. "Areas of Human Activity." *Journal of Educational Research* 30:672-79. (May 1937).

Gagné, Robert M. *The Conditions of Learning*. New York: Holt, Rinehart and Winston, 1970.

————. "Some New Views of Learning and Instruction." *Phi Delta Kappan* 51:471 (May 1970).

Gattegno, Caleb. *Towards a Visual Culture*. New York: Outerbridge and Dienstfrey, 1969.

Gerberick, J. Raymond, Green, H. A., and Jorgensen, A. N. *Measurement and Evaluation in the Modern School.* New York: David McKay, 1962.

Gerlach, Vernon S., and Ely, Donald P. *Teaching and Media: A Systematic Approach.* Englewood Cliffs, N.J.: Prentice-Hall, 1971.

Gillespie, John T., and Spirt, Diana L. *Creating a School Media Program.* New York: Bowker, 1973.

Gronlund, Norman E. *Constructing Achievement Tests.* Englewood Cliffs, N.J.: Prentice-Hall, 1968.

Gross, Ronald, ed. *The Teacher and the Taught: Education in Theory and Practice from Plato to James B. Conant.* New York: Dell, 1963.

Gross, Ronald, and Osterman, Paul, eds. *High School.* New York: Simon and Schuster, 1971.

Haberman, Martin. "Behavioral Objectives: Bandwagon or Breakthrough." *Journal of Teacher Education* 19:91-94 (Spring 1968).

Hamreus, Dale G., ed. *Media Guidelines: Development in Validation of Criteria for Evaluating Media Training.* Washington, D.C.: Bureau of Research, Office of Education, U.S. Dept. of Health, Education, and Welfare, June, 1970.

Harvard Committee. *General Education in a Free Society.* Cambridge: Harvard Univ. Pr., 1945.

Helvey, T. C. *The Age of Information: An Interdisciplinary Survey of Cybernetics.* Englewood Cliffs, N.J.: Educational Technology Publications, 1971.

Herriott, Robert E., and Hodgkins, Benjamin J. *The Environment of Schooling: Formal Education as an Open Social System.* Englewood Cliffs, N.J.: Prentice-Hall, 1973.

Hertzberg, Hazel W. *Historical Parallels for the Sixties and Seventies: Primary Sources and Core Curriculum Revisited.* ERIC Microfiche, ED 51-066.

Hicks, Warren B., and Tillin, Alma M. *Developing Multi-Media Libraries.* New York: Bowker, 1970.

Hockett, Ruth Manning. *Teachers' Guide to Child Development: Manual for Kindergarten and Primary Teachers.* Sacramento: California State Department of Education, 1930.

Holt, John. *What Do I Do Monday?* New York: Dutton, 1970.

Hug, William E. "Are You Philosophically Consistent?" *Science Education* 54:185-87 (Apr.-June 1970).

———. "Promising Alternatives to Current Educational Practice." *Southeastern Librarian* 23:18-21 (Summer 1973).

———, ed. *Strategies for Change in Information Programs.* New York: Bowker, 1974.

Hussain, Khateeb M. *Development of Information Systems for Education.* Englewood Cliffs, N.J.: Prentice-Hall, 1973.

Jensen, Arthur R. "Understanding Readiness: An Occasional Paper." *Challenge* 1:6 (Nov./Dec. 1972).

Joyce, Bruce, and Weil, Marsha. *Models of Teaching.* Englewood Cliffs, N.J.: Prentice-Hall, 1972.

Katz, William A. *Introduction to Reference Work. Volume 1: Basic Information Sources.* New York: McGraw-Hill, 1969.

Kaufman, Robert A. *Educational System Planning.* Englewood Cliffs, N.J.: Prentice-Hall, 1972.

Kelley, Earl C. *Education for What Is Real.* New York: Harper, 1947.

Kemp, Jerrold E. *Instructional Design.* Belmont, Calif.: Fearon, 1971.

Krathwohl, David R., ed. *Taxonomy of Educational Objectives, Handbook II: Affective Domain.* New York: David McKay, 1964.

Liesener, James W., and Levitan, Karen M. *A Process for Planning School Media Programs: Defining Service Outputs, Determining Resource and Operational Requirements, and Estimating Program Costs.* College Park: School of Library and Information Services, Univ. of Maryland, 1972.

Lyle, Guy R. *The Administration of the College Library.* New York: H. W. Wilson, 1961.

Mager, Robert F. *Goal Analysis.* Belmont, Calif.: Fearon, 1972.

————. *Preparing Instructional Objectives.* Palo Alto, Calif.: Fearon, 1962.

Mager, Robert F., and Pipe, Peter. *Analyzing Performance Problems or 'You Really Oughta Wanna.'* Belmont, Calif.: Fearon, 1970.

Martin, Lowell A. *Library Response to Urban Change.* Chicago: American Library Assn., 1969.

McLuhan, Marshall. *Understanding Media.* New York: McGraw-Hill, 1964.

Melcher, Daniel. *Melcher on Acquisition.* Chicago: American Library Assn., 1971.

Mesarovic, Mihajlo D., ed. *Views on General Systems Theory.* New York: John Wiley, 1964.

Miller, Van, Madden, George R., and Kincheloe, James B. *The Public Administration of American School Systems.* New York: Macmillan, 1972.

Mize, Joe H., White, Charles R., and Brooks, George H. *Operations Planning and Control.* Englewood Cliffs, N.J.: Prentice-Hall, 1971.

NEA Commission on the Reorganization of Secondary Education. *Cardinal Principles of Secondary Education.* U.S. Bureau of Education Bulletin No. 35. Washington, D.C.: Gov. Print. Off., 1918.

NEA Educational Policies Commission. *Education for ALL American Youth.* Washington, D.C.: National Education Association, 1944.

The National Special Media Institutes (NSMI). *The Affective Domain.* Washington, D.C.: Gryphon House, 1972.

————. *The Cognitive Domain.* Washington, D.C.: Gryphon House, 1972.

————. *The Psychomotor Domain.* Washington, D.C.: Gryphon House, 1972.

Oettinger, Anthony G., and Zapol, Nikki. "Will Information Technologies Help Learning?" *Teachers College Record* 74:5-54 (Sept. 1972).

Phenix, Philip H. "The Architectonics of Knowledge." In *Education and the Structure of Knowledge.* Stanley Elam, ed. Chicago: Rand McNally, 1964, pp. 44-74.

Popham, James W., and Baker, Eva I. *Planning an Instructional Sequence.* Englewood Cliffs. N.J.: Prentice-Hall. 1970.

President's Commission on National Goals. *Goals for Americans.* Englewood Cliffs, N.J.: Prentice-Hall, 1960.

*Principles and Practice of Instructional Technology Workbook.* Palo Alto, Calif.: General Programmed Teaching, n.d.

*The Pursuit of Excellence: Education and the Future of America.* New York: Doubleday, 1958.

Redden, J. D., and Ryan, F. A. *A Catholic Philisophy of Education.* Milwaukee: Bruce, 1942.

Rugg, Earle. *Curriculum Studies in the Social Sciences and Citizenship*. Greeley: Colorado State Teachers College, 1928.

Sarason, Seymour B. *The Creation of Settings and the Future Societies*. San Francisco: Jossey-Bass, 1972.

Saylor, J. Galen, and Alexander, William M. *Curriculum Planning*. New York: Holt, Rinehart and Winston, 1966.

School Library Manpower Project. *Behavioral Requirements Analysis Checklist*. Chicago: American Library Assn., 1973.

————. *School Library Personnel Task Analysis Survey*. Chicago: American Association of School Librarians, 1969.

Sereno, Kenneth K. *Foundations of Communication Theory*. New York: Harper and Row, 1970.

Shannon, Claude, and Weaver, Warren. *The Mathematical Theory of Communication*. Urbana: Univ. of Illinois Pr., 1949.

Smith, Alfred G. *Communication and Culture*. New York: Holt, Rinehart and Winston, 1966.

Smith, Hayden R. "Media Men Arise: What If McLuhan Is Right?" *Educational Screen and Audiovisual Guide* 47:18-19 (June 1968).

Smith, B. Othanel, Stanley, William O., and Shores, J. Harlan. *Fundamentals of Curriculum Development*. New York: Harcourt, Brace, 1957.

Steinberg, Charles S. *Mass Media and Communication*. New York: Hastings House, 1966.

Stetler, Rose E. "An Experiment in Informal Education." *California Journal of Secondary Education* 10:516-17 (Nov. 1935).

Swarthout, Charlene R. *The School Library as Part of the Instructional System*. Metuchen, N.J.: Scarecrow, 1967.

Taba, Hilda. *Curriculum Development: Theory and Practice*. New York: Harcourt, Brace and World, 1962.

Thelen, Herbert A. "The Triumph of 'Achievement' over Inquiry in Education." *Elementary School Journal* 60:190-97 (Jan. 1960).

Tickton, Sidney G., ed. *To Improve Learning: An Evaluation of Instructional Technology*. Vol. I. New York: Bowker, 1970.

Tosti, Donald T., and Ball, John R. *A Behavioral Approach to Instructional Design and Media Selection*. Albuquerque: Behavior Systems Division, Westinghouse Learning Corp., 1969.

Tracey, William R. *Designing Training and Development Systems*. New York: American Management Assn., 1971.

Travers, Robert M. W. *Man's Information System: A Primer for Media Specialists and Educational Technologists*. Scranton: Chandler, 1970.

Trump, J. Lloyd, and Miller, Delmas F. *Secondary School Curriculum Improvement*. Boston: Allyn and Bacon, 1968.

Ulich, Robert. *The Human Career*. New York: Harper, 1955.

Ullmer, Eldon J., and Stakenas, Robert G. *Instructional Development Handbook*. Tallahassee: Florida State Univ., Division of Instructional Research and Service, 1971.

Vickery, B. C. *On Retrieval System Theory*. Hamden, Conn.: Archon, 1965.

Wilsberg, Mary Elaine. "Effective and Ineffective Teacher Behavior as Viewed by Teachers in a Team Teaching Situation." *Dissertation Abstracts* 26:2606 (Nov. 1965).